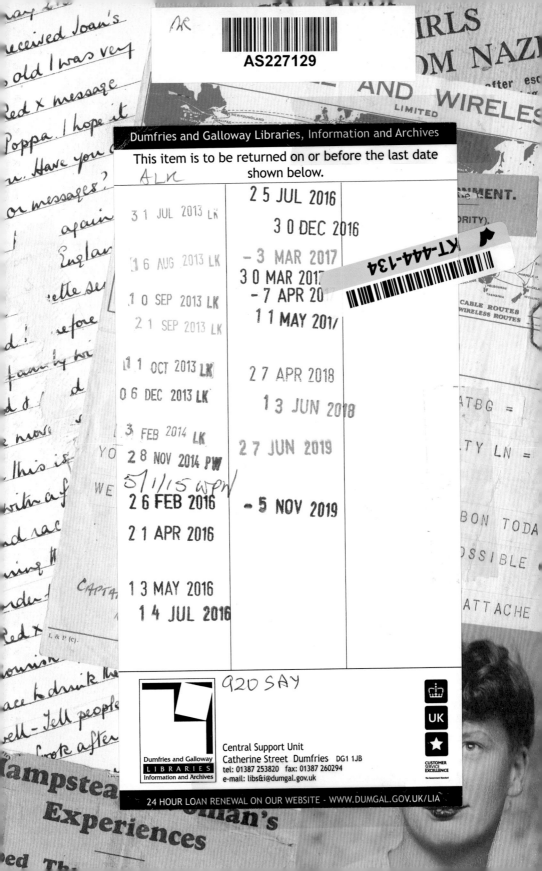

ROSIE'S WAR

Rosie's War

AN ENGLISHWOMAN'S ESCAPE
FROM OCCUPIED FRANCE

ROSEMARY SAY & NOEL HOLLAND

Michael O'Mara Books Limited

First published in Great Britain in 2011 by
Michael O'Mara Books Limited
9 Lion Yard
Tremadoc Road
London SW4 7NQ

A CIP catalogue record for this book is available from the British Library.

Papers used by Michael O'Mara Books Limited are natural, recyclable products
made from wood grown in sustainable forests. The manufacturing processes
conform to the environmental regulations of the country of origin.

ISBN: 978-1-84317-557-5

1 2 3 4 5 6 7 8 9 10

www.mombooks.com

Cover design by Geoff Haye

Designed and typeset by K.DESIGN, Winscombe, Somerset

Printed in the UK by CPI William Clowes Ltd, Beccles, NR34 7TL

Contents

Prologue

'Oh, come on, Mum! We're nearly finished now. Surely you must remember how you reacted?'

Silence.

'Look. Think back. You're an English girl. It's June 1940. You're standing on the Champs-Elysées and the German army's marching right past you into Paris . . .'

More silence.

'You must have reacted. Why doesn't your generation seem to feel anything?'

Mum looked at me. She wasn't going to react. We were having tea in her North London flat while we talked about her wartime escapades in France. She had asked for our help in setting it all down in a book. But I think she was fast beginning to regret involving us – her daughter and son-in-law – in anything to do with her story.

'Well,' she said, giving my husband a big smile, 'I fancy some wine. How about you two?'

'Bloody stonewalling, Mum. Don't just ignore my questions.'

I could keep on protesting but I knew it was all over for today. My mother was a determined woman. The very experiences we were writing about had made her a lot tougher than me. If she decided that she did not want to express her feelings then that was that.

I watched her struggle to her feet and walk over to the kitchen. She was a tall woman in her late seventies, bent low by the onset of Parkinson's. But you could still clearly see the active and slightly ungainly girl who smiled out from the wartime photographs that were spread out on the table in front of us.

She had started to write down her story before she became ill. We had offered to help her complete it, asking questions and fleshing out the rough draft. But, as usual, our efforts to explore further were reaching a stalemate. We didn't seem to be able to get any deeper into her life or thoughts. Most sessions would end like this one, with me getting frustrated and fast reverting back to petulant adolescence, my husband being a bit embarrassed and my mother becoming annoyed at my strident tone. Hence her offer of a drink as a way of ending the interview.

I am old enough to have parents who experienced the Second World War as adults. Like many other children of my generation, I grew up on their wartime stories.

In my mother's case, these adventures were particularly dashing. She was trapped in France after the German army had invaded that country in 1940, was imprisoned in a German-run camp in the east of France and escaped to England in the middle of the war. She subsequently worked in Spain for the glamorous and secretive Special Operations Executive until a scandalous romantic entanglement led to her being sent back to England.

These tales were all part of our family myth. They had become a series of funny episodes that helped to explain some of the eccentricities of my mother's character. Why did a quiet family weekend away, for example, mean at least six complete changes of clothes, enough food for a week and several large emergency items (I remember a plastic washing-up bowl on one occasion)? Why did she have an almost pathological hatred of being left in the dark right to the end of her life?

And how had she acquired an encyclopaedic knowledge of nineteenth-century French literature? She had certainly never formally studied the subject.

Memory plays tricks. At this late stage in her life my mother could not always disentangle myth from reality and often she didn't want to. She had honed her stories over the years. She had literally dined out on them for more than half a century. They might be delivered before the pudding or after someone else's tale. Her aim would be to produce from her listeners the appropriate responses of amusement or awe. Historical accuracy was not necessarily so important.

In this way, the long passage of time had turned the coherent events of a little over three years in the life of a young girl into a series of humorous but mostly unrelated cameos. My mother loved being seen as a great character and she certainly had the life stories to match. Her war escapades were the high point. Like most children, I simply accepted the stories, having heard them hundreds of times. It was not until we began to write them down that I realized how complex is the relationship between memory and truth. On a simple level, my mother would confuse key wartime facts or dates, even when she was using them to explain or remember her own experiences.

The death of the actor Leslie Howard is an example. When she escaped from the German prison camp and travelled across Europe, she had real difficulty in getting a seat on a flight to Ireland from Portugal. Why? Because Leslie Howard had been killed on the same route just a few weeks previously, his plane having been shot down by the Luftwaffe. At least, that was my mother's explanation. It was not until after her death that we checked the facts: Howard's fatal crash was actually a year later. Yet my mother had been certain for over half a century that the crash had been in some way the reason for her problems in getting a flight.

Stress or panic alters memory. In my mother's account there are at least thirteen Saturdays to a month. She seemed to talk of everything happening on a Saturday. This meant that throughout her escape and travels she was continually being blocked and frustrated by shops closing early or offices not open. Yet again the curse of the weekend, she would moan! But when we checked the dates we found that this had happened only once or twice. Just often enough to leave a recollection of such panic that it coloured all her reminiscences.

Memories are personal possessions. But once you tell them to others they are out there to be used. I remember her indignation at finding her own stories being purloined for someone else's autobiography. 'How would she know that? She was never around the camp at the time. I told her that story after the war when I was working at *The New Statesman*.' Such was her typically caustic comment on one woman's so-called autobiography. That particular book is sitting on the shelf in front of me as I write this.

Feelings were rarely present in what my mother recounted. Her tales were all about action and events. Emotion would only surface when she felt that someone else had borrowed her remembrances for their own ends. Yet her story was that of a young woman, with all the self-doubt, introspection and emotion of youth. Exciting or amusing adventures are all very well but they only explain what happened, not why something happened.

'Weren't you scared when you saw the Germans marching into Paris? Or exhilarated? You were only yards away from them.

'Why did you leave it until June 1940, when Hitler was practically on your doorstep, before you tried to get home to England? Didn't you want to be with your family at such a dangerous time?'

These were the sorts of questions that my mother simply refused to answer. Many of her background and generation – a middle-class girl born in 1919 – refuse to analyze or even acknowledge their motives and feelings. Maybe this was the way it had to be. Perhaps the war generation managed to survive and be so brave precisely because they didn't try to explain or rationalize. The same phrases recur in their memoirs: 'You just did it'; 'It was expected of you'; 'No one questioned it'; 'I just happened to be there'; 'Anyone would have done the same'.

It's all so self-effacing, so relentlessly cheery, so matter-of-fact. Any attempt to probe further or to dig deeper is dismissed with a casual remark: 'Oh, I don't know about that . . . Now, shall we have another drink?'

Perhaps we underestimate the impact of signing the Official Secrets Act. That signature covers you for life, not just until you finish your job. If you can't talk about significant events when they happen, you withdraw over time even from your own past. That was certainly the case with my mother.

Just take a glance at the Colditz escape accounts of Pat Reid or Airey Neave. Watch the wartime films of John Mills. Or marvel at the cheery Kenneth More playing the part of the terribly injured Douglas Bader. All phlegmatic. Distant. Detached.

Such reticence came up again and again as we talked to my mother and her friends and read autobiographies of the time. You feel as if you only ever hear half the story. The person seems to be recounting someone else's life, not their own. There is a tremendous remoteness and coldness in the tale.

For us – the therapy generation – such detachment may be understandable but we still want more. We not only want to tell the tale, we also want to explain it.

My mother died before we could finish this account together. She told us all she was able to. This story is the result of her memory and our bullying.

PART ONE

An Englishwoman Abroad

JANUARY 1939 – DECEMBER 1940

CHAPTER ONE

Departure for France

Late October 1938. A blustery, mid-autumn morning.

I was at a job interview, sitting by the window in a rather shabby, second-floor office of the National Union of Students in central London. I was waiting for some further comments from the lady who was interviewing me, a Miss Coulter. In the meantime, I had quite a good view out of the corner of my eye of the buses crawling down to the Aldwych.

Miss Coulter was elderly and fastidious. She had been silent for quite a time, her lips pursed as she read through some documents piled on her desk. She seemed to shift a little uneasily in her seat.

Had I said something wrong?

I had been trying to sound eager but not desperate. Perhaps I had overdone it and she simply thought that I was either slightly mad, or naïve, and she wasn't sure how to break the news to me.

I had applied through her organization to go and live in Germany, working as an au pair. Perhaps my choice of location seemed a bit strange, given that we had nearly been at war with that country just a few weeks before. I wasn't totally ignorant. I had seen the trenches being dug in Hyde Park – a primitive sort of air raid shelter – during the crisis over Czechoslovakia. I had witnessed the panic in London. But, like the majority of ordinary people, I didn't think war would ever come. Nothing would interfere with my life.

'Well, Miss Say,' Miss Coulter said at long last. 'I don't think that we'll be able to help you in your specific request.' She smiled somewhat patronizingly. 'I'm sure you appreciate that we can't really encourage any young person to go to Germany at this particular time.'

She shuffled her papers and looked up at me. I nodded and stared at her rather blankly. I was beginning to feel a bit foolish and embarrassed by the whole procedure. After all, I wasn't a student, I knew nothing about looking after children and I barely spoke French, let alone any other European language. I felt she knew all this and was politely trying to let me down.

'What about France?' she asked after another long silence.

'I beg your pardon?'

'Well, we could try to place you in France instead of Germany.'

'That's fine with me.'

She looked a bit startled by my ready agreement. I felt like telling her that I would have agreed to go to China if she had told me that it was a good idea. I simply wanted to get away from London and from my family.

Let me give you a little of my background.

I came from a solid, middle-class family. We lived just off Hampstead Heath in North London. My father, a former naval officer, had a comfortable job in the City. He and my mother were Edwardian in outlook, with entirely traditional aspirations for their three children. So, while my brother David had gone up to Cambridge to read theology, I had enrolled on a secretarial course in central London with my older sister Joan.

I was now nineteen years old and had been working for the past year as a secretary at a catering college near to where we lived. It was a large, austere building which reminded me of school, with long, grim corridors where a domestic always seemed to be polishing the floors. It even smelt like school: soap and watery food. I had a very comfortable if rather predictable existence at home. I willingly gave half of my thirty-five shillings a week wages to my mother. I suppose I didn't really have much need for money: I walked to work where I had food provided, had no desire to save for the future and was paid for at the cinema, the theatre or restaurant by my boyfriend Bobby.

Bobby was part of the problem. He was just too right: ten years older than me, good-looking, our parents firm friends. He was in the process of taking over his father's auction house in Lisson Grove. It was a business that he would in the future make very successful. On a couple of occasions he had even selected items of furniture for me at the showroom after a night out in town. Our relationship was a settled one and I suppose everyone assumed that we would eventually marry. But it was all very chaste and unexciting.

My great passion was poetry. I took myself very seriously here. I filled notebooks with my own attempts, diligently writing something every day as practice for the future. A rather precious and intellectually arrogant young woman, I would walk the short distance up to Hampstead High Street to hear the major new poets reading their work. I remember listening with rapture one evening as a young W.H. Auden read aloud.

Poetry was even the cause of rows between my mother and me. She rejected poets such as Auden and MacNeice, for example, on the grounds that they were vulgar. Her strait-laced attitude merely strengthened all my feelings of being misunderstood.

I was bored with my safe and predictable life: I wanted out. I longed to dance the light fandango and be silly. It wasn't that I meant to make trouble for my family, but rather that I didn't want to go on placating my mother while feeling absolutely mean about how tired I made her. She was a tall, thin woman who always seemed to find life an effort. She had had me at the then advanced age of thirty-four. I had been sent off to boarding school (unlike my siblings) at the age of seven because

I was too energetic and noisy. She still seemed to find me too much to cope with.

I had decided earlier in the year that I had to do something different and radical that would break the mould being set for me. But what? It wasn't until early that autumn, walking over Hampstead Heath one bright, cold afternoon with my schoolfriend Peggy, that I decided exactly what I would do.

'I'm going to live abroad,' I declared.

'Where? How will you live?'

'Oh, I don't know. I haven't got that far yet.'

'But what will your parents say?'

I looked at Peggy and shrugged my shoulders. The truth was that I had decided on what I was going to do but as yet had no idea of how I would do it. We walked around Highgate Ponds discussing which country I should go to and how I might support myself. All the potential destinations were carefully dissected. After her initial scepticism, Peggy became much more enthusiastic about the whole scheme.

'My uncle went to Argentina years ago,' she said. 'He works for a British railway company there. Perhaps he'd help.'

'No, it's too far. I don't fancy weeks at sea.'

'Look, if you're really serious about going somewhere in Europe, why don't you write to the National Union of Students? My brother has one of their booklets. I'm sure it says they arrange trips for young people on the Continent.'

We went back to Peggy's house to look at the pamphlet. She was right: the NUS could arrange so-called educational visits for students in Europe, lasting anything from a month to one year.

So, a few days later I settled down to write a long letter to the NUS. I told them that I wanted to go to Germany, giving a lot of spurious reasons for my choice. I remember that one of the more preposterous ones was that I was hoping to be able to hear the famous existentialist philosopher Heidegger lecture at Freiburg University.

My letter must have appeared a bit ridiculous but I can only think now that I felt the need to sound intellectual. After all, this organization was for students, yet I had left school at sixteen and had no hope of going to university.

Why did I choose Germany? Well, I had already ruled out anywhere outside of western Europe. I didn't want to be too far from my parents after all. But which country then? I had been put off France by my school experience of trying to learn its language. Spain was in the midst of civil war. Germany was perhaps the obvious candidate. I knew a little of the country, having spent a couple of weeks there in my early teens with the Girl Guides. Even in the late 1930s it was easy to focus more on its wonderful cultural achievements of the past than on the actions of its present Nazi government. Yes, our countries might go to war at some point, but that would surely be in the distant future and not during my brief stay there? Anyway, of more importance to me than the choice of country – Germany or France – was the fact that I was going to be living abroad sometime soon.

At the end of November a letter arrived from the NUS suggesting a family in Avignon, in the South of France. It appeared that their present au pair, a Miss Sylvia Story, had to return to England at Christmas and they were looking for a replacement. There were three small children.

I showed the letter excitedly to Peggy that evening. She was distinctly underwhelmed.

'An au pair is a general dogsbody. You'll be sweeping the floors. You should hold out for a job teaching English at a school.'

'Well, I think I'll talk to the present girl when she gets back before I decide anything.' I was annoyed by her reaction. I wanted her to be enthusiastic. It would help me keep my nerve.

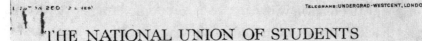

TELEGRAMS:UNDERGRAD-WESTCENT, LONDO

THE NATIONAL UNION OF STUDENTS

OF THE UNIVERSITIES AND UNIVERSITY COLLEGES OF
ENGLAND AND WALES.

Federated to the International Confederation of Students.

3, ENDSLEIGH STREET,
LONDON, W.C.1.

BC/BMO

28th November, 1938.

Miss R. Say,
42, Pattison Road,
Hampstead, N.W.2.

Dear Miss Say,

    One of our students who is staying 'au pair' with a family in Avignon has to return to England at Christmas, and as this family want someone else I have told them about you. The English girl who is there now is called Sylvia Story, and it is very probable that you will hear from her.

    The family in question consists of the father, who is an engineer, the mother and three children - two boys aged 5 and 10 and a girl aged 3. The duties of the post are to give the mother some help with them, and give instruction in English. You would be received as a member of the family, have a separate bedroom, opportunities for learning French, and of course a certain amount of free time. Miss Story has been very happy in Avignon, and I think you would enjoy the post. Before anything definite can be decided about this post, the family wish her to interview any applicants, and as she is coming back to London shortly, I shall be glad to arrange for you to see her.

    The family would like to see one of your snapshots, and I should be glad if you would let me have them as soon as possible. I shall also be interested to hear when you have a letter from Miss Story.

        Yours sincerely,

A.R. Coulter

Secretary for Exchange and Tuition Visits.

Rosie's letter from the NUS.

I met Miss Story just before Christmas. We arranged to have coffee one morning at a hotel in the West End of London. She bounded into the lobby laden down with Christmas shopping. She was tall and slim. Her hair was cut into a delightful bob and her clothes were elegant. I couldn't help wondering whether France would have the same effect on my appearance.

She told me that she had been happy with the family, the Manguins, and described them as gay and delightful. She had been with them for nearly a year but was now returning to England to look after her mother. I did not warm to her. She seemed very bossy and controlling, advising me in no uncertain terms how long I should stay with the Manguins (one year at most) and exactly what work I should be prepared to do. Nevertheless, her obvious possessiveness of the job made me think that the family must be nice. They wanted their replacement to arrive about the second week in January. That settled it for me. I would be abroad early in the New Year.

The night of 9 January 1939 I lay in bed quietly going over all the arrangements in my mind.

I was leaving for Avignon in the morning. At last the family discussions were behind me. My parents had been very cooperative once they had got over their initial shock. Perhaps I should have suspected an element of relief on their part, but if so I was much too taken up with my own plans to worry.

I had some money. Bobby had given me a few French francs. My father, with all sorts of careful warnings about overspending, had presented me with £2 (the equivalent of a little over £80 today). I had carefully locked away the money in one of my new suitcases.

These were the pride of my life. They were made of pale, buff pigskin and were incredibly heavy even when empty. They had my initials stamped on the top in gold. Unlike my school trunk, which bore the name Pat Say, these suitcases proudly proclaimed the owner as

Rosemary Say. My father had given me the name Pat after he had returned from sea to be presented with a new baby daughter. 'Rosemary's too beautiful a name for her,' he had declared as he looked at my unprepossessing face. 'We'll call her Pat.' So Pat it was until my suitcases changed all that. My parents had given them to me as a leaving present and I was convinced they were all I needed to complete my new chic French image. The fact that I couldn't carry even one of them very far didn't worry me in the least. Travel in those pre-war days always entailed porters and trolleys.

It was a very loaded-down porter's trolley that carried my suitcases onto the Paris train at Victoria Station the next day. All the family, including Bobby, had come to see me off.

From the photos of the occasion, the scene looks almost Edwardian: my mother tall and elegant in a full-length fur coat; my father, brother and Bobby all in large-lapelled suits and overcoats, wearing Homburg hats and carrying rolled-up umbrellas. My brother David towers above everyone. There's no avoiding the unmistakeable Say teeth – protruding and prominent – in David, Daddy and me. My mother has a slightly anxious expression on her face. In contrast, I look so excited and happy. I had finally got what I wanted and couldn't wait to begin. I can hardly turn round to face the camera: I am simply bursting to be gone.

'Are you sure you know how to change stations in Paris?' my father asked for what seemed to be the twentieth time.

'Of course I do. Don't fuss, Pa. I have reserved seats all the way through. It's a very simple journey.'

I felt much too excited to worry about any travel details. I wanted to hug and kiss my family but I also wanted to go, to escape and begin my adventure. I already felt detached from my past life, friends and relatives.

'Have a lovely time, Pat. See you on your birthday.' My mother kissed me on the cheek.

I got onto the train. Leaning out of the window I said goodbye to Joan and David. I blew Bobby a kiss. 'Cheer up. I'll be back in March for my birthday.'

'See you then, Pat,' he shouted, blowing a kiss back to me.

'Bye, Pat, bye-bye!'

The sounds of my family stayed with me as the train began to pull away through South London. I looked out of the window at the flat suburbs. So here I was, just two months short of my twentieth birthday. I had some money and was going to be paid a wage in France. I certainly had no apprehensions. On the contrary, I felt confident about the future and my abilities to deal with life.

I am naturally an optimist and always believe I can get the hell out of a situation if I don't like it. After all, hadn't I decided after tea one day (at the mature age of seven) that my carefully selected boarding school was not the place for me? I was found that evening with my bags at the front gates and taken to the headmistress. I calmly explained to her that as I didn't like her school I now wished to go home.

Surely if I didn't like my new life in Avignon I could leave just as easily?

I did, in truth, have some fears as I left London. But they were not profound, more immediate and prosaic. How much should I tip the porter? Could I steel myself to go into the dining car alone? What would the waiters think of me?

In fact, I didn't dare go into the dining car. I don't know what or how I ate on the eighteen-hour journey from London to the South of France. But I do know that my lack of French kept me awake: in particular, I remember worrying on the journey south from Paris about how you pronounced the 'g' in Avignon.

Years later my elder daughter asked me what was I expecting or dreaming would happen in France. I suppose she saw me as a sheltered girl of only nineteen going out into the unknown by myself. What were my hopes, my expectations?

I couldn't really answer her. Of course, I had the usual romantic daydreams about falling in love. But perhaps the most important thing for me was that at last I was going to be an individual. No longer the youngest and least satisfactory part of a large family or a boarder at school, but simply a young Englishwoman working and living in Avignon.

I had finally gained my independence and was starting my life.

CHAPTER TWO

Settling Into Avignon

'Avignon! Avignon! Mademoiselle! Réveillez-vous! On arrive!'

The guard brusquely woke me up.

The train ground to a halt. I looked out. It was dark and cold. Wearily, I collected my belongings and set them down on the platform. There was no one there to meet me. An elderly porter approached and silently took my bags. I was still very dozy.

Suddenly I remembered my suitcases in the guard's compartment. I tapped the porter on the back.

'Monsieur! Er . . . mon . . . suitcase. En tren!'

I pointed towards the train.

Damn! What was the French word for suitcase? I couldn't remember! I frantically started to draw large squares in the air with my hands and jab at the train. The porter looked bemused. He smiled and nodded but did nothing.

'More,' I shouted. 'There are more cases. Encore. Plus.'

My French was breaking down completely. At last he seemed to understand, but it was too late. The train hissed and steamed away to Marseille.

I was nearly in tears. I was tired and my beautiful suitcases had disappeared. Why did I have so much stuff when I couldn't even get it out of a train?

'Êtes-vous Mademoiselle Say?' said a man who had by now arrived on the platform. He introduced himself very formally as Monsieur Claude Manguin, my new employer.

He had very little English but quickly understood my distress. With some rapid instructions he arranged with the porter to have my cases sent back from Marseille.

We drove off through the winter air around the great medieval walls of Avignon, journeying in complete silence. I was too tired and shaken by my disastrous attempt at speaking French to the porter to try to make any small talk. Anyway, judging by the look on his face, the last thing Monsieur Claude wanted was a hesitant conversation about my journey. He probably hadn't relished getting out of bed in the early hours of the morning to collect the new au pair from the station. He was a short, stocky man of about forty, with a head of receding slicked-back hair. He looked very determined and was perfectly polite but remote, driving fast and smoking cigarettes all the way.

I was relieved when we arrived at a countrified and quite unpretentious villa just outside the town. Madame Odette Manguin was waiting to meet me. She quietly showed me to my room so that I could have a few more hours of sleep.

When I awoke later that morning I found that I was in a neat, pretty room that in some indefinable way could never be English. Maybe it was just the light, which even in January had a yellow glow to it, utterly unlike the hard grey of a London winter morning.

Miraculously, my precious suitcases had already arrived. I got up and began to unpack, pulling out clothes to wear that day. I hurried downstairs to find Madame Odette and her children still at the breakfast table.

'Good morning, Pat. Pour yourself some coffee and come and sit down.' She smiled and pointed me to an empty place at the table.

'I hope you managed to get some more sleep. You'll find that everything starts very early in this house. Monsieur Claude left for work an hour ago.' She spoke French very slowly and clearly with almost no trace of a Midi accent.

'Thank you,' I replied gratefully. Gulping the coffee, I looked across the table at the three children who were watching me unblinkingly.

'Bonjour,' I said. 'Tell me your names.'

'I am Henri,' said the eldest in English. He was tall and slim, with fine features and brown hair swept elegantly away from his forehead. A real ladies' man for the future, I thought.

'Pleased to meet you, Henri.'

'But my friends call me Biquet,' he continued. 'I am ten. I like playing ball and swimming. Don't you think my English is good?'

'Very good.' I smiled. 'I can see that you will have to teach me French.'

He smirked. Perhaps it was at the wonderful thought of him being the teacher. It struck me that I might have some trouble with him. Very spoilt. He continued by introducing me to his siblings, pointing first to the little blonde girl with ringlets who was intently chewing on a piece of toast.

'This is Catherine. She's five and she likes ballet.'

Well, that seemed very clear. I began to think through what I could remember from my own ballet crush at the age of eight.

'You will have to show me all your dancing steps after breakfast.'

Catherine smiled but said nothing. She couldn't understand me.

'And this is my brother Jean-Pierre. He's seven and his ears hurt.'

The little boy was wonderfully sweet. He had a thatch of fair hair set on a wide face. His two top front teeth were missing, giving him a goofy smile. He nodded his head politely.

'Oh dear,' I said, looking towards Madame Odette.

'Don't worry,' she replied, patting Jean-Pierre on the head. 'He has mastoids in cold weather but I find a good, thick cap keeps the pain away.' She rose from the table.

'Now come along, Biquet,' she said. 'It's time for school and we have to show Pat the way. She will collect you this afternoon. You two can come as well.' I don't think that the younger children were very keen on accompanying us to school but they obediently trooped after their mother.

So began my new life with the solid, bourgeois Manguin family. I would settle quickly into the household, with the children choosing the nicknames of Patoun and Meese for me.

Monsieur Claude, the son of quite a famous artist, was a commercial traveller for a chemicals firm selling *potasse d'Alsace* (potash). He would start for work early each morning to visit his local customers. He was a busy man of few words and I was to have little to do with him.

His wife was very different. She was not considered a proper Manguin, coming as she did from Paris. She was amusing, talkative, intelligent and unflappable. She was to become my security over the months ahead.

Madame Odette was also very elegant. She was probably in her mid-thirties but to me she seemed much younger. Dark haired, immaculately groomed and with beautiful make-up, she had perfectly shaped eyebrows that might have belonged to a film star.

Compared to her, I felt all the clumsiness of my tall, big-boned body. I was not fat, far from it, but I was very athletic with a large frame and a big bust. I still had all the energy and awkwardness of a schoolgirl who hasn't quite come to terms with her body. Unlike Madame Odette, my movements were gawky and ungraceful. I was certainly, despite my smart suitcases, the antithesis of French chic.

Within a couple of days of my arrival, Madame Odette took control of my wardrobe. She went through all my clothes, seemingly as a matter of course.

'Patoun, what is this colour?' she said, holding out my treasured suit that I had recently bought with such pride in the Marshall & Snelgrove sale.

'Cyclamen,' I said weakly.

'Yes, ma petite, I know what it is.' She smiled at me pityingly, as though at a rather feeble-minded child. 'But how can the English do this to such lovely material?'

I had little defence. The colour was dreadful. She put a number of my outfits on the bed.

'We'll dye these dark blue, Patoun. If you could buy two packets of dye before you fetch Biquet we can do it first thing tomorrow.'

I did what she asked and a few days later we went to Madame Simone, the dressmaker in town. She did what she could with the shape. My transformation was underway.

As for the three young Manguins, my first impression of them had been correct: they were very well behaved and would prove easy to look after. My initial reaction towards Biquet had also been right: he was certainly spoilt. But I found that I could keep him under control with the threat of reporting any misdeeds to his father. It was Jean-Pierre who quickly became my favourite. He was a delightful little boy, always very worried about being teased over the large woollen hat that completely hid his ears.

My duties as an au pair were not exactly onerous. I was expected to get the children up in the morning and dress them. At night I bathed them and put them to bed. Taking Biquet to and from school was one of my main duties. The two younger children often accompanied us on these trips. I was also expected to give Biquet piano classes of a sort and daily English lessons.

There was no general housework to do, as Peggy had promised there would be. Madame Odette was far too organized to need a rather inept English girl to help her run the house. At most I would be asked to do some mending.

The two younger children were left very much to their own devices during the day. I would sometimes be asked to keep an eye on them. This proved an easy enough task once I had enlisted my mother's support from London. Throughout that first winter a steady stream of cards and children's books arrived, much to the delight of Jean-Pierre and Catherine. The latter, in particular, was thrilled to find out the names of the seven dwarves in English. 'Atchoo, non. Sneezy, oui,' she would say delightedly to anyone who would listen.

Apart from these tasks, the time was largely my own. I knew few people, especially of my own age. It was quite a lonely existence but I was content with this. I would spend much of the day reading on my bed, from where I could look out on to the apple orchard below. A couple of times a week I cycled into town for an afternoon matinee at one of the cinemas, with only a scattering of other people to keep me company in those vast, art deco buildings. At the weekends I would play tennis across the river at the sister town of Villeneuve lez Avignon or mix with the Manguins' friends who came to supper. But I had little in common with these people who were, for the most part, much older than me. My evenings were often spent babysitting.

My only real friend was Simone, the Manguins' maid. She was a tall girl with curly, black hair and a prominent forehead. She was a little younger than me and came from Aix-en-Provence. She was very lively and loved teaching me the local slang, the more obscene the better. We would laugh and giggle as I practised new words in make-believe conversations around the house. She claimed to have a boyfriend living in Marseille who was involved in the criminal underworld. I don't know how much of this I believed but it was good fun to listen to.

I was given a massive, old-fashioned bicycle known in the family as *La Reine Marie* (Queen Mary), on which I would attempt to cycle round town. One of my favourite mental pictures of that time is of Jean-Pierre desperately hanging on to my back as I struggled against the attempts of the ferocious mistral wind to blow us into the river.

The bicycle was also to be the cause of my brush with the Avignon underworld. This was not quite in the Marseille league but to me it was still terrifying. One particularly cold, snowy day I went into Avignon to run some errands for Madame Manguin. I lost control of my bicycle in one of the narrow, winding streets of the centre. As I struggled to keep it upright I knocked over an old woman. I was alarmed and ran back to see how she was. Instead of a feeble, gentle, old lady who needed reassurance and help, I was faced with an angry virago demanding money or she would report me to the police for reckless behaviour.

I was in a dilemma. I had very little French and no wish to confront a policeman who might ban me from the roads and thereby make it impossible for me to take Biquet to and from school. I felt like the heroine of a nineteenth-century novel, blackmailed over her terrible past. I gave in. For several weeks I would meet this old woman on a Friday morning and pay her to keep quiet.

Reason eventually returned to me and I simply stopped going to meet her. For the first few days I waited for her to denounce me, hardly daring to go out and certainly not on my easily recognizable bicycle. But nothing happened. She obviously realized that the worm had turned and was off looking for some other mug.

My main problem during the first few months in Avignon was that of language. Reading was not the issue. I was near enough to the discipline of my own schooldays to find it easy to sit down and do exercise after exercise. I would spend hours with both English and French versions of books such as Balzac's *Le Père Goriot*, translating one language into the other and back again. I read French literature voraciously and indiscriminately.

But speaking was another matter. I had to get rid of my hesitant schoolgirl French and start speaking if I wanted to belong in the country. It seemed to take me about ten minutes to think of something to say at the meal table and then I would often come out with double entendres that would make people howl with laughter. 'Merci, je suis tres excitée de venir avec vous' ('I am very aroused to be coming with you'), was a classic that left me red in the face at one Sunday lunch.

As for Avignon itself, I had not expected it to be exotic and I was certainly right about that. It was a beautiful, medieval, walled city with lots of cafes and squares. The old Palais des Papes dominated the northern end with the famous Pont d'Avignon beside it. But it was still a very small, provincial place. For a London girl such as myself who was used to a big city, it was like Canterbury perhaps. And even then I wasn't living in the centre but in a pleasant, quiet suburb. It was all slightly dull and tranquil.

I suppose I might have become bored with this somewhat uninspiring town and quiet routine had it not been for our long holiday visits to stay with Monsieur Claude's father on the Mediterranean coast.

Père Manguin, as he was affectionately known, had a large house on the outskirts of St-Tropez. He was a painter of the Fauve school. This was a post-impressionist movement from the beginning of the twentieth century that emphasized vibrant colours and bold brushstrokes. Matisse, Marquet, and Derain had been among his Fauvist contemporaries and friends.

After the great experimental days of his youth, however, he seemed to have had no desire to explore the world further. Perhaps this was a result of his being more comfortably off than his fellow artists. Consequently, his later reputation would not measure up to those who went on to other discoveries. Today he is largely forgotten. Nevertheless, when I got to know him his work was still being shown all over the world and he seemed to receive colossal sums for it.

Père Manguin was a wizened man with a shock of white hair. He accepted me into his household seemingly without much enthusiasm. Perhaps he just thought of me as a rather ungainly, prissy English girl with little charm or wit. Or maybe it had something to do with my second day at the villa, when I had gone to the lavatory during the sacred post-lunch siesta and had dared to pull the chain. Roaring out from his room as the pipes rattled and thundered round the house, he told me what he thought of idiotic English girls. I took the children down to the beach for the rest of the afternoon.

In those days St-Tropez was not really much more than a fishing village. After the war it was to be made famous by Brigitte Bardot but at that time it was dominated by the widow of Paul Signac, the Pointillist painter. Around her was grouped the cultural set. The poet Léon-Paul Fargue had a sharp, bitchy wit – 'the evening was agitated by Paul Poiret's hand,' as he once described a party at the house of the great dressmaker who had Parkinson's disease. Ambroise Vollard was there, the art dealer who had made plenty of money by snapping up early Cézannes, much to the disgust of Gertrude Stein. The artist Édouard Vuillard (of the complicated pattern paintings) would often be around with his elderly friend and fellow painter Ker-Xavier Roussel, who would rather reluctantly join us all for a swim in the sea in a laughably tight rubber bathing cap. And the writer Colette would slump in, I don't know from where, with her perpetual query to me: 'Tu as vu mes chats, petite anglaise?' ('Have you seen my cats, little English girl?')

Sometimes they all sat around the large table in the garden looking down at the beach and the sea across to St Raphael, the sunlight playing on the big white tablecloth. The conversation (as much as I could catch of it) was animated, violent and voluble. I was terribly impressed by them. As I wrote to my father, 'They are serious and cultured people . . . Their friends are gay enough but they make a clique of Paris life which can only be joined after real hard work and success.'

One day Père Manguin's model failed to turn up. His wife, Madame Jeanne, was not available to sit for him. She had some business to attend to in town.

'Et pourquoi pas, Patoun?' she suggested to her husband.

He looked at me, snorted in disgust and muttered some comments about Englishwomen. Picking up a bowl of fruit from the table he went off to his studio to do a still-life painting.

A few days later, however, I was sitting on the beach with the children when the old man's voice came from behind ordering me not to move. After being frozen for what seemed like hours, I was at last allowed to get up.

'There,' he said, handing me the picture to look at. 'That is an English back.'

He stomped away without another word. I wasn't sure if he meant this as a compliment but I was pleased to have made the grade as a model.

It was early in my second visit to his house in August 1939 that I finally broke the ice with this daunting figure and his family. I remember the moment precisely. We were seated at the dinner table on the large verandah overlooking the bay. The darkness had come down and the evening air was gentle and cool. The last train had rattled beneath us, taking the workmen home from the torpedo factory near by. As the conversation continued around me I had my perpetual concern: what could I say to amuse or even interest them?

'Tell us about your family,' said Madame Jeanne, turning to me with a smile. 'Étonne-nous, Patoun.'

I gulped in desperation.

To me there was nothing exciting to say about my family that would surprise her, as she wanted. As I saw it, we were a rather staid, middle-class lot. There was an elder brother who had been at Cambridge and who was now an ambitious cleric; an elder sister in a secretarial job; my mother at home; my father, a reserve naval commander who worked in the City . . .

'Ton père,' said Monsieur Claude. 'Que pense-t-il de Monsieur Churchill?'

'Beaucoup,' I said lamely. There was bemused silence at the table. 'Mon père porte un monocle de temps en temps,' I volunteered in despair.

In truth, it was only on very rare occasions that I had seen my father using a monocle. Nevertheless, I mimicked him putting it to his eye and looked around the table rather fiercely. Everyone laughed, much to my surprise. Biquet began to copy me. 'Je suis Monsieur Say,' he said as he went around the table, peering at the members of his family rather pompously through his imaginary monocle.

I suddenly realized that with this small and innocuous gesture I had at last opened the door to the Manguins' affection and interest. From now on I was to be accepted as part of the family. I was *drôle*, a character. Farewell the gauche English girl who always seemed at a loss for words. No longer would Père Manguin threaten me with his gun when he was 'fishing' with bullets from the window of his studio. And now conversations at the dining table would often end with 'N'est-ce pas, petite anglaise?' To be happy was to sit on the right hand of French approval. 'N'est-ce pas, petite anglaise . . .?'

This small episode proved to be the turning point of my life in France. Having struggled for over half a year with speaking the language and adapting to the culture, I suddenly achieved self-confidence in both. From then on I began to love every minute of my new life. It seemed to me that this relaxed, undaunted lifestyle was truly living. The long meals where everyone was relaxed and witty were attractive and fun. It was so different from the carefully planned and tense entertaining of the English middle classes, with my mother frantic from having got up at six in the morning to start preparing the house and food for guests. I had no desire to shine in these French meals, just to be accepted. I was very happy.

As I wrote to my parents, 'French life suits your daughter exceedingly well . . . this enterprise is turning out completely successfully.' I was now fearless even with the language. One evening towards the end of that second holiday I organized a small play with the children based on the French subjunctive. For some reason (inexplicable at this far remove) I found the conjugation both fascinating and hilarious. I assumed that the audience would as well. Much of the play was based on stilted sentences starting with phrases such as 'Il faut que je fasse.' I don't know how Père Manguin and the family reacted to this. With polite bemusement, I suspect.

A boyfriend was still the one thing I lacked for most of my time in Avignon and St-Tropez. There was, of course, the devoted Bobby in London who sent me gramophone records and news from home. Somewhat unfairly, I kept him going all the time without any promise for the future. He came over to see me at Easter, not long after my arrival, and we met in Paris. But it was terribly boring, walking the streets of the city without much to say to one another.

It was not until I had been in Avignon for over a year that I had a boyfriend. He was a serious-minded teacher of maths called Patrice. Tall and with a very angular face, he would hold my hand nervously, trying to tell me how much I meant to him. I suppose that he was part of the reason why I was reluctant to leave Avignon when the war began in earnest for us that spring.

I have often been asked over the years why I didn't leave earlier. After all, I was in Avignon from January 1939 until June 1940 and France was at war for over half that time. Why did I leave it until absolutely the last minute to get out, indeed just days before France collapsed?[1]

One reason is that virtually none of my acquaintances talked of the possibility of war during my early months in Avignon. Perhaps such problems were not taken seriously in the Midi of France, traditionally so detached from Paris both emotionally and psychologically. 'Let the Parisians get themselves worked up,' seemed to be their attitude; the Midi did not concern itself with such affairs of state. Of all the people I knew, Monsieur Claude was alone in growling his prophecy that we should all be saved by Monsieur Churchill when the time came.

My lack of concern during those early months about any future war may also have been due to the fact that I led quite an isolated life. I knew few people of my own generation and no one who was called up to serve in the armed forces. I knew no English people in Avignon or St-Tropez; if I had I might have seen them preparing to go home. So I was not in an atmosphere of panic or worry. When I discussed the war and speculated along with everyone else about what was going to happen, it was as a young French girl from the Midi that I was thinking. However, there was more to it than this. In my dreamy way I was refusing to face the truth until the last possible moment. I simply wanted everything to turn out all right.

There was also the matter of losing face with my family. I didn't want to be proved wrong in my decision to go and work in France as an au pair instead of choosing a more traditional pre-marital path for a middle-class girl. I was always conscious of the fact that my very conventional parents compared me unfavourably to my older sister

---

[1] Germany was at war with Britain and France from September 1939 but there was hardly any fighting that winter of the so-called Phoney War. The following spring, however, the German blitzkrieg campaign saw its army overrun much of Western Europe in a few weeks.

Joan, who was ensconced in a good job in London and soon to marry an ambitious naval officer. I certainly did not want to return to London having seemingly failed in my French adventure. As I wrote to my parents in August 1939:

> I understand that you must be wanting to see me safely installed – and if one can look into the future with any certainty – Hitler and God permitting – I'll arrive somewhere in the end even if by a slower and more irregular route than Joan and in a different line.

CHAPTER THREE

France at War

*I*t was only when France was merely days away from war that the seriousness of my situation finally dawned on me.

The family spent what was in many ways a very normal holiday in August 1939 at Père Manguin's. I was looking forward to seeing my brother David, who was planning a visit at the very end of the month. One evening before dinner I wandered down to the beach and saw warships in the bay. An old man stood there watching them.

'La guerre arrive,' he said, shaking his head sadly. 'La guerre arrive.'

I watched him staring fixedly out to sea. The sight of the warships in that beautiful bay – their sheer size and dull colour menacing the bright little sailing yachts and fishing boats – made the prospect of war very real and immediate. I looked at the old man and thought of my father. His generation had already survived the Great War. It must have seemed unbelievable to them that war was about to engulf Europe again.

Monsieur Claude called me aside a couple of days later. He looked ashen-faced. It had just been announced on the radio that Germany and the Soviet Union were about to sign a non-aggression pact. I slowly began to understand that this meant war for France and Britain. As he explained, Hitler could now turn his attention to attacking the West without having to look over his shoulder at the Soviet Union.

Certainly the pact seemed to shake everyone in the Midi out of their lethargy. Two days later I wrote to my parents: 'The situation internationally is now the first subject of everyone's conversation.' I began to hear that lots of foreigners in St-Tropez were making hasty plans for departure.

Monsieur Claude, who was a captain in a reserve regiment, received a telegram ordering him to report to his unit the following week. He sped back home to Avignon that very afternoon, returning to St-Tropez a few days later at 3 a.m. (he didn't have permission to leave his barracks) to pick us all up. The children grumbled sleepily in the back of the car about this abrupt change in plans. Their father explained to them that he had work to do. The parents tried to appear cheerful but I could detect real concern under the surface.

We arrived back to a very different Avignon from the one we had left less than a month before. The town was already teeming with soldiers on the move. We saw off Monsieur Claude the next evening at the station; his unit was being dispatched north. The scene was like the photographs of Victoria Station in 1914, with every carriage of the train packed with troops and military equipment.

What was I to do now? I wrote to my parents of the need to be realistic: 'To gaze at the proverbial blue Mediterranean only means watching perpetual manoeuvres in the bay with bombers roaring overhead.' But what was realistic or advisable at this point? I didn't know where I would be safer if the German bombers started their campaign – London or Avignon. Or even if I could reach England if I decided to go home.

I discussed what to do with Madame Manguin but before we could reach any firm conclusions the decision was taken out of my hands by the fast-moving events of the following days. By Sunday, 3 September 1939, Britain and France were at war with Germany.

There was a real sense of panic during those days. There were rumours of mass evacuation away from the dangers of the nearby armaments factory. Housewives were already beginning to hoard food, as whispers of rationing spread. Just two days before the war started, I dropped a quick note to my parents, written hastily at the post office:

Working hard as house in dreadful state – all Avignon to be evacuated because of nearness of powder factory . . . The telephone for private calls is cut and a telegram takes three days unless official! . . . Trying to buy sugar – <u>impossible</u> to find anywhere.

I could not have returned to England in September 1939 even if I had wanted to. With the armed forces being mobilized, the travel situation in France during those first few weeks of war was chaotic. I explained in a letter home to my distraught parents:

There are no seats on the trains now, and no regular times, nothing but troops moving all the time . . . travelling conditions are not really possible for me alone, whatever the English authorities say.

The German invasion of Poland lasted only a matter of weeks. This surprisingly swift victory added to my confusion over whether I should stay or go. Everyone I talked to in Avignon fully expected England to be invaded at any moment. This was surely no time to return? My letters home were now more concerned with my family's safety back in England than with my own in France: 'You should get out before the inevitable aerial onslaught,' I pleaded.

My parents thought otherwise. Once the war had started they wanted me home and they continued to worry about me throughout the period of the Phoney War. In October my concerned father enlisted the support of the British Consul in nearby Marseille, a Mr Norman King.

This gentleman wrote me a rather pompous letter, stating that he was in full agreement with my father that I should return forthwith to

England, especially given that train services were now running again quite regularly. His Majesty's Government would offer me any financial assistance needed, he added. Like a rather stubborn and naughty child, I wrote back saying that for the present I was not leaving but would (of course) obtain the necessary visas if and when I decided to go.

I was secretly rather impressed by the fact that the letter and envelope were stamped with the royal cipher. It certainly had the effect of making me begin the lengthy process of ensuring that my papers were in order – endless forms, stamps and payments – so that I could leave the country when necessary. I understood my parents' concerns. I made a promise to write a postcard to a member of the family every other day on the even date. Needless to say, this commitment was never kept.

Just how differently my parents and I viewed events, living on either side of the English Channel, was summed up by my polite thanks to them for having filled in my ration forms. There was 'nothing like that here yet'. I continued: 'Your taxes and rationing are necessarily stiffer than out here, where life is not so dear, but each day there seems to be another restriction or expense for you – still our time is coming!'

As it turned out, of course, hostilities weren't to start in Western Europe in earnest until the following year. Life in Avignon returned to a sort of normality after the first few weeks of panic and confusion. It seemed that large-scale war might be avoided after all. 'The Anglo-French firm outlook is a ray of hope,' I wrote to my father. I settled in France ever more comfortably during that winter. Monsieur Manguin's absence in the army brought some financial problems for the family and they could no longer pay me. But this was a blessing in disguise, as it forced me to take on private English classes. I was soon saving money for the first time in my life. I had mastered the French language by now and even had vague plans to move to Paris the following autumn to start studies at the Sorbonne. And, most importantly, by early 1940 I was in love with Patrice.

Why go home under these circumstances? As I put it in a letter to my parents:

> I am busy and individual here, which suits me better than to be thrown into the melting pot of National Service – perhaps I am wrong – anyway I am happy. With the help of the consulate and authorities who are friends I shall manage perfectly all right when I want to leave.

I did, however, rather hesitantly explain that I would need some money to tide me over. As advised by Mr King, I had applied for and obtained a *carte d'identité*, costing 300 francs. I promised my father that from now on I would go easy on spending any more money.

My life in Avignon was one of complacency and calm during that first winter of war. I even went over to London in March 1940 for my twenty-first birthday celebrations. In hindsight it seems extraordinary that I was allowed to travel back to France in mid-April and that my family and I considered it appropriate. After all, the Germans attacked Denmark just a few days before I was due to leave London; the war had now started for real in Western Europe. Nevertheless, the trains were all running normally and for me the only slight strangeness was the fact that I now needed a visa to travel to the Continent. There was certainly no sense of panic or urgency either in England or France. None of us could foresee that France would collapse so completely and spectacularly within a few weeks.

I think too that I so desperately wanted everything to be all right that I refused to see any dangers. All my letters home over those months, whatever the content, sound so happy. I was constantly reassuring everyone that I was fit and healthy, enjoying for the first time a way of life that totally suited and fulfilled me. It is difficult now to think of any other explanation for my travelling back to France on 17 April, less than a month before the Germans invaded the Low Countries.

The events of the few weeks following my return to Avignon soon shook me out of my stubborn complacency. The war began in earnest for France in the second week of May. The rapid advance of the German army through the Low Countries and Northern France stunned us all. Horror stories about German atrocities began to circulate. As I cycled back from school with Biquet one warm afternoon at the end of May, I saw a car arrive with a mattress on its roof, holed with machine-gun fire. The boy thought this an amusing sight but I was horrified. Reality had pushed its way into my little dreamy world and I was frightened.

That evening, when the children had gone to bed, I discussed with Madame Odette what I had seen.

'It's the first of the refugees from the north. They're fleeing from the fighting. We'll soon be awash with them.' She paused and looked at me directly. 'Patoun, have you given any more thought as to what you should do?'

'Well, yes. I don't think I can go on like this. I'm being such a worry to my parents and to you. Everything's moving so quickly and I don't think they can cope with much more.'

She nodded in agreement. 'You can't put off your decision for long. It might soon be impossible to get home.'

'I know I have to decide on something quickly but I don't want to get it wrong. What if I go and it turns out to be safer here?'

'We'll miss you, Patoun,' she said, getting up from her chair and coming over to kiss me on the forehead. 'No one really knows what's for the best but you must just do what you think is right.'

I hardly slept that night, worrying about my future plans. I knew that the Manguins were planning to move to a large house outside Avignon with another family. I also knew that my parents would be relieved if I went home. And at the back of my mind was the daunting prospect of looking after eight young children in the new house, instead of the usual three. On the other hand, I felt that people shouldn't be going to London but leaving it. I was really concerned about my parents staying on there. I wanted them out. 'My concern for you is a sincere sentiment quite detached from anything else,' I wrote.

By the following morning I had made up my mind. I decided to send a telegram home telling them that I was returning to England.

And so I began the cumbersome business of organizing my travel and visa, with endless telephone calls to the nearest British Consulate in Marseille and to Southern Railways in Paris. On top of all this, my private pupils had to be informed that I was leaving. All the while Madame Odette still wanted help with the children and with the sorting out of the clothes, furniture and various personal possessions which went with the closing down of the house. She had no idea when they would be returning nor under what circumstances.

In the midst of all this I received another letter from Mr King, the British Consul in Marseille. He was giving what he said was his 'final' advice. He now believed that travelling at the moment was too difficult and uncertain. The only port left open was St-Malo, which was hundreds of miles away in the north-west of the country. Even if I managed to reach it, he added, I might be stuck there indefinitely, praying that a boat would soon be leaving for England. If I really wanted to leave France, the best way would be for me to take a plane from Marseille. But the whole situation was very uncertain and no one could give me any guarantees.

At £15 a ticket (over £600 in today's money) the plane seemed sheer extravagance, the very thing I had promised my father not to indulge in. I didn't even know if I could get a seat. As I explained to my worried father that same day, Saturday 7 June:

If neither you nor I are in immediate danger it is rather exaggerated. Don't worry that it is so difficult to get back – in case of emergency I can always manage but this time it seems better to wait a bit.

Even at that late stage (the Germans were to be in Paris within the week) we were unaware of how feeble the Allied military effort really was. In the same letter I wrote: 'If only we can keep up this resistance and no one else betrays us!' Perhaps the ease and speed with which I was still getting post from England also misled me as to the seriousness of the situation. I petulantly complained about not receiving any word from my brother and cousin, especially since 'letters from London only take a week to arrive now.'

On Monday 9 June I received another letter from my father. He, of course, was still expecting my return to London. He informed me that he had also received a letter from Mr King, who had told him that 'Your daughter may apply to me for any assistance of which she may stand in need.' In a typical Pat move I then decided to hedge my bets and find out about the possibility of a seat home on a plane. I telephoned Mr King's office, gave my details to the receptionist and asked to be put through to him. To my utter amazement I was told that he had already left for England.

'Can I speak to someone else about the best way to get back home?' I asked.

'Wait a moment, Miss Say,' said the woman on the other end. Did she notice the note of real concern and shock in my voice?

I suddenly felt rather foolish. Until now I had been so sure that I had time to consider my options and work out what to do. But I had just learned that the British Consul – no less – had already fled. Why was I worrying about spending money on air fares or wondering what people might think of me? Why was I carefully trying to decide what I should do? It was surely time just to get home.

After a long pause a man came on the line. He asked my whereabouts and continued speaking without waiting for a reply.

'It's useless to go to Bordeaux. There are thousands of people fighting to get on the available boats. And down here all the transport is already reserved, I'm afraid.'

BRITISH CONSULATE GENERAL

MARSEILLES

22-3S/40
JM.PD

1st June, 1940

Sir,

I am in receipt of your letter dated May 24, regarding your daughter Miss Rosemary Say and have to inform you that her address has been noted and that she may apply to me for any assistance of which she may stand in need.

I am, Sir,

your obedient servant,

H.M.CONSUL GENERAL

Lieut.Comdr. R. Say R.N.V.R
   c/o Admiralty
      Whitehall
         S.W.1

British Consul's letter to Rosie's father offering assistance.

Reserved for whom? I wondered.

'Hold on, Miss Say. I'll transfer you to another desk. They might be able to offer some assistance.'

Another pause. Then yet another voice.

'Miss Say? Look, why not take a train to Paris? You can slip through to Rennes and then make your way to St-Malo. That port is still open. You should stand a chance of finding a boat to England from there.'

With that telephone call I was to start my long journey home of nearly two years. The fatuous piece of advice to 'slip through' the advancing German lines to the north-west coast of France has haunted me ever since.

In hindsight I can't think why I didn't consider heading down to Nice, the other port on the Riviera from which British citizens were being evacuated. I later found out that the British Consul there had checked all his registered flock and carried out his duties before leaving for England. But at the time there seemed no alternative to travelling to Paris. I was frightened by the gravity of my situation. I was also intimidated by the voice of authority. At twenty-one years of age, I didn't realize that authority is not an all-powerful divinity that handles every crisis with absolute efficiency but that it is made up of fallible individuals.

I telephoned Avignon station immediately and arranged a seat on the train for the following day. The family gave me a wonderful farewell dinner that evening. I remember plenty of champagne and my boyfriend Patrice at the piano, playing Chopin beautifully.

The following day I went to the station with Madame Odette and the three children. There was chaos as we got near. Our taxi crawled along, trying to avoid the people who thronged the road. Whole families were wandering about, burdened with possessions. They looked lost and bewildered. At the station there was a huge crowd blocking the entrance. They had no luggage with them: they were simply waiting for their loved ones to arrive. We struggled out of the taxi just as the train coming south from Paris pulled into the station. It was absolutely packed. The passengers streamed off in relief, most looking around anxiously to see who was meeting them.

The noise and the press of the crowd were intense. The arrivals were embraced with relief and joy by their relatives and friends. Little Jean-Pierre was knocked over by a large lady in a fur coat. She only had eyes for her husband and certainly not for the child, whose nose was left streaming with blood after coming into contact with her handbag.

A young officer saw our distress and offered to help me with my suitcases. The Manguins left me at the ticket barrier. It was madness for them to try to get any further. The officer used my suitcases as battering rams to push his way through the crowd to the platform. It turned out that he was catching my train as well. We had to wait only a few minutes before it arrived from Marseille.

It was 11 June 1940. The German army was on the outskirts of Paris. The previous night (we later learnt) the Prime Minister and his Cabinet had fled the capital, heading south-west to the Loire. Although I did not know it at the time, I had the rather dubious distinction of catching probably the last train northwards to Paris in the history of the Third Republic.

Talk about lamb to the slaughter. I had almost begged for the knife.

CHAPTER FOUR

Paris and the American Hospital

I sat in my carriage and looked out at the chaos. The crowds were still on the platforms, presumably waiting for the next train from the north and some sign of their loved ones. The heat of the late afternoon was intense. We stayed in the station for what seemed an age, finally setting off in the dark of the evening. There were very few of us on that stuffy train travelling northwards. I chatted with the other occupants of my carriage. There was a family visiting friends in Lyon – in retrospect, perhaps a curious thing to be doing at that particular time. There was also the young officer who had helped me. He was returning to his regiment from leave.

I dozed through the long hours of the night. But any sleep was fitful, as I was aware of the train constantly slowing, stopping and starting up again. As I looked out in the misty dawn light I had my first glimpse of the reality of mass flight. Every time the train travelled next to or over a road or stopped at a station I saw a steady procession of people moving south, towards the place I had left.

Cars were jammed against each other. Prams, trolleys, carts and tired horses trundled along or were pushed with a resigned doggedness. I saw what looked like whole farms loaded onto carts: pots, pans, children, chickens, pigs and calves all mixed up together. There was a silence, a conserving of energy.

Even more eerie in that mass of desperate people was the sight of the roadsides strewn with all manner of things: dead pigs and horses, household possessions and broken-down cars. There were pieces of furniture that had been precious enough to take on the journey south but were now abandoned, just pushed to the side of the road and left. There were cars that had been packed with so much luggage and so many people that they were stranded with their axles ruptured. Children were running between groups of women, their cries the only sounds in all that herd of people. I was told later that many children were simply lost in the huge exodus.

For a moment I panicked. Was it sheer madness to travel towards the approaching German army just as thousands of terrified people were fleeing from them as fast as they could? I looked at my two big suitcases on the rack above me. I also had various other possessions up there, including a hatbox and some parcels and bags. I surely wouldn't be able to carry everything if I got off now and joined these people.

So that decided it: I stayed on the train. Perhaps it was also the fact that I felt safer there. Just as you don't actually feel part of the landscape as it flies past your window, so I couldn't really connect with those people trundling south. It was as if I was merely an observer of their terrible plight and suffering. I had been told what to do and I was concerned that I would be lost if I joined that extraordinary spectacle of frightened people on the move. No one would know where I was. In Paris, at least, someone would surely be responsible for people like me.

By now we had left Dijon and were well on our way. The young soldier was the only other occupant. He was probably in his mid-twenties, not much older than I was. He told me his name was Joseph. He had intense blue eyes, black hair and sallow skin.

We talked in a desultory fashion. We were both distracted but for different reasons. I was concerned that I was making a mistake in going to Paris. I couldn't take my eyes off the crowds on the roads still pushing their way southwards. The image of an old woman being wheeled along in a handcart was so harrowing that it stayed in my mind.

Joseph, by contrast, seemed to be quite unconcerned by what was going on outside. He told me he was worried about his mother who was dying of cancer. He had just been to see her, almost certainly for the last time. He was now returning to his unit north of Paris. He didn't even know if it would still be fighting by the time he reached it. There were all sorts of rumours swirling around that the French government was going to sue for peace.

Our conversation had run its course. He rose and jammed his heavy kit bag up against the carriage door. The blinds were still down, so no one could see in from the corridor. He sat next to me and gently lowered me on to the carriage bench without a word being said. We made love. It was brief, perfunctory and almost totally silent. We both felt comforted.

The last part of the journey was interminable, as we crawled through the southern suburbs of Paris. We were halted at the level crossings by the sea of human misery trying to escape from the German army. People simply took no notice of the train, which had to inch its way through the teeming crowd. Many were using the railway tracks to walk south, slowly and painfully getting out of the way of the oncoming train.

When I had left Avignon the scene at the station had been one of chaos: bewildered and relieved arrivals meeting the mass of nervous, expectant people waiting desperately for news. But this was nothing in comparison to what I saw at the Gare de Lyon in Paris. It was utter pandemonium. There were hundreds, perhaps thousands, of frantic people pushing, shoving and shouting to get on our train for the return journey. They were demented, fleeing for their lives. Well before we reached the platform they were boarding the train through the doors and windows, pushing possessions and children in ahead of them.

For a while I almost doubted that we'd be able to get off. As in Avignon, Joseph used my heavy suitcases to shove his way through the crowd. We struggled out of the station. I was anxious to get to the British Embassy but couldn't face making my way there with my luggage. Joseph suggested that we went to a nearby bar, where he asked the patron to look after my suitcases for a while.

'I don't know which of us faces the greater tragedy,' he said. 'Sois courageuse.' ('Be brave.') He kissed me and departed.

When I arrived at the embassy I found that the British authorities had left Paris the night before. There was a note pinned to the door advising those of us who were left behind to seek help at the US Embassy. With a rising sense of panic I asked a passing old man how to get there, saying that I was English. He explained briefly. He then crossed himself.

'Que Dieu vous protège,' ('May God protect you.') he said.

The streets were very quiet. There was no sound at all. I walked past the Café de Paris which was one of the few places open. I sat alone on its terrace while attentive waiters served me coffee, bread and fruit. I was worried about my luggage and decided to return to the bistro where I had left it before trying to find the US Embassy. The large and rather greasy-faced patron was there by himself, polishing glasses. He smiled at me.

'You can leave your things here for a while. They'll be safe. They say that Paris is going to be declared an open city.'

I looked at him quizzically.

'Meaning, Mademoiselle, that there'll be no fighting. The German army will be allowed to march in unopposed.'

I nodded but really had nothing to say to this.

'Even so, don't wander around the streets too much. Use the Métro while it's still open. It's safer.'

Just then I heard dull thuds of gunfire. I ran to the window. Great pillars of smoke were rising up into the peerless blue sky. He chuckled.

'We're blowing up the fuel storage depots before the Germans arrive.'

'Why?'

'They'll be here in a few hours. We don't want the bastards to help themselves to free fuel, do we? They'll have everything else in the city, though.' He spat on the floor rather melodramatically.

'The politicians have already left and the *deux cents familles*.[2] They've made sure that they're safe. Most of us ordinary people are trying to get out today.'

'And what about you?'

'Some of us have to stay.'

Why? Was it simply out of concern for his property? And what of his family, I thought, noticing his wedding ring.

He tapped the highly polished brass counter and sighed. 'Don't go out yet, Mademoiselle, you'll get covered in soot from the fires. Sit down and have a cognac.'

He poured drinks for both of us and got on methodically with his work. I sat at the bar and sipped my drink. I wasn't used to spirits and the cognac burnt my throat. It began to calm me down after a few minutes but I was still desperately worried about my situation and in a state of nervous excitement.

As I sat there, watching the soot raining down, I heard the first of the loudspeakers booming out: 'Young men, save yourselves. Go quickly.' I later learnt that this was the first open cry of the collaborationists telling the youth of Paris to make their way by whatever means to the Brittany coast. It was a despicable measure

---

[2] A reference to the Bank of France's 200 largest shareholders (who represented virtually all the great French families). Until 1936 they were the only shareholders allowed to vote in its General Assembly. There was a widespread feeling that the country was effectively run by these families.

designed to lower morale. Ironically, of course, it was precisely what I had been intending to do.

After a while the air seemed to clear a little. I got up, thanked the patron and hurried off to the US Embassy. When I arrived there I was directed to a side entrance. Inside there was a long queue of people, presumably most of them British. I got talking to the person in front of me, a Mr Parsons. He was a middle-aged man from Hastings who had settled in Paris after the Great War, working as a sales rep for a British textiles company. He told me that his French wife and children had travelled to his parents in England the week before. He was now desperate to follow them.

We stood in the queue for a number of hours. This pleasant man filled me in on the motley selection of British nationals who were waiting resignedly to hear what was to become of them. A group of Protestant nuns stood ahead of us. They were from a convent just outside Paris, he explained. The few stranded travellers dotted around were quite easy to pick out. There were a number of local British residents like him, most of whom he seemed to know. We were truly the odds and sods of Paris.

I finally managed to see an embassy official. He was a slight, young man of about thirty with an extremely harassed look on his face. He was obviously out of his depth here. After all, what was he supposed to do with all these people? I came quickly to the point.

'I arrived in Paris from Avignon this morning. I have no idea what to do now.'

'Why on earth did you come up from the south?' He looked at me incredulously.

'Well, the British Consulate in Marseille advised me to go to Paris and then to slip through to Rennes,' I explained defensively. 'They said I could go on to St-Malo from there and get a boat to England.'

'Slip through?' he snorted. 'Slip through what? The German army? That man in Marseille is mad.'

'Oh, it wasn't the Consul himself who told me this. He'd already left when I telephoned.'

My words sounded more and more feeble. Tears began to stream down my face. The young official looked embarrassed; I don't know if this was a result of his outburst or of my response. He peered down at the papers on his desk.

'It's too late to get out now, Miss Say. There's no way of organizing transport. The German army is just outside the city. It'll be here in a few hours.' He flicked through a pile of papers on his desk and pulled out a sheet.

'Look, why don't you try the American Hospital at Neuilly? You're young and they might be able to fix you up with something. But you'd better hurry. There's already a crowd trying to get jobs.'

He scribbled an address for me on a piece of paper, smiled briefly and beckoned to the next person in line. I got up and left quickly. There must have been at least thirty people behind me still waiting to see him. I clutched at the straw that he had given me. I had heard of this hospital: it had a reputation as one of the most expensive nursing homes in Europe.

I was desperate to get there but my first thoughts on leaving the embassy were for my luggage way over on the other side of the city. Would it be safe? I suddenly woke up to reality. What did my luggage matter? Those suitcases had dominated my life since leaving Avignon. I hadn't dared leave the train because of them. I had arrived late at the US Embassy because I needed to check with the patron that they were safe. Enough. I was trapped in Paris with the German army on its doorstep. I had nowhere to stay that night and no means of supporting myself. I needed to get to Neuilly as soon as possible.

Coming out of the Métro, I walked in the blazing sun along big avenues and past enormous houses which were shuttered and deserted.

There wasn't a sound on the streets. Everyone had gone from this rich and elegant quarter of the Paris suburbs. I walked on alone, searching rather frantically for the hospital. I was acutely aware that I had only 650 francs in my pocket (just over £150 in today's money). How long would this last me if I couldn't get a job?

I was still feeling slightly lightheaded from the cognac; it had been a few hours since I had sat in the bistro with the owner and had eaten nothing since then. I saw a small girl sitting on a step playing contentedly with her doll. A while later a British sailor went drunkenly by, humming to himself.

I found the hospital at last. It was a huge turn-of-the-century building with a wonderful, curved driveway leading to the entrance. There was a large and very un-English queue of people jostling and shouting. I joined them. The late afternoon sun was still hot and after a while I started to doze on my feet. I was rudely shaken out of my dream-like state by a harsh voice.

'Well, what can you do, girl?'

I looked up to see the most enormous woman glaring at me. Matron. She seemed like an absolute sod. And indeed she was, as I was to discover.

'Oh, most things,' I stammered. 'If I put my mind to it.'

I smiled at her. I must have seemed very hearty and jolly. She gave a sort of snort and nodded.

'Well, collect a uniform down the corridor. The nurse there will tell you what to do.' Without another word she marched away.

I was a bit dazed. Why had I been chosen out of the crowd? I didn't dwell for too long on this question and hurried off down the corridor. Within a few minutes I had been fitted out with a striped blue dress, crisp white apron and white cap.

A rather distracted staff nurse told me my duties. I was to be a *fille de salle* or chambermaid: scrubbing, swabbing down and polishing the long corridors during the day and helping out in the doctors' dining room in the evenings. I could sleep on the couch in the staff flat of one of the nurses nearby. There would be full board but no pay. I was to start work the next day at 5.30 a.m.

On my second day at work I was told to report to the office of the hospital administrator, Mr Edward Close. He was an American with a beaming face and a jovial manner. He was apparently very popular with his staff but I found him rather slimy and took an instant dislike to him. He sat at his desk and rapidly took down my details and background. When he had finished he put away his pad and turned to me.

'The German army is entering Paris as I speak. But rest assured, Miss Say, not a hair on your head will be touched.' I wasn't particularly reassured by his words and merely nodded.

'Are there any other English people here?' I asked him. 'I'd like to see them if there are. If that's possible, of course.'

I simply wanted to talk to an English person. I couldn't say precisely why. Perhaps it might give me a sense of security. Mr Close shifted in his seat a little uneasily and referred to some papers on his desk.

'Yes. There are three British servicemen here. But I can let you see only one of them. The others are too badly injured.' He scribbled a room number on a piece of paper which he gave to me.

'But watch your step, young lady. I'm expecting the German High Command any day and I don't want anything out of order.'

I thanked him and hurried out. Before returning to work I went to the canteen to snatch a quick cup of coffee. A young American doctor approached me.

'Hey, you're the new English girl, right? Do you want to go downtown to see the German army arriving? The truce has just been signed. They're coming in.'

'Yes, all right. But could we stop first near the Gare de Lyon to pick up my luggage?'

'Sure.' He smiled.

'What about Matron?'

'Oh, don't worry about the dragon. She's already taken off to see them. Come on!'

We set out in his car with three other American doctors. The transport system was now closed down and I was relieved to be able to collect my possessions. Apart from anything else, I desperately wanted some clean underwear. When we got to the bistro the patron was relieved to hand over my suitcases. He seemed wary, fearful even. Perhaps not surprisingly, for harbouring English luggage could no longer be considered a friendly act and might lead to reprisals.

We hurried off and parked in a spot specially reserved for Americans just by the Arc de Triomphe. I sat on the car roof looking across at a German military band playing on and on as we waited for the parade to begin.

When it finally started it was a most amazing sight. The powerful war machine rolled down the Champs-Elysées: gleaming horses, tanks, machinery, guns and thousands upon thousands of soldiers. The procession was immaculate, shining and seemingly endless. It was like a gigantic, grey-green snake that wound itself around the heart of this broken city, which was waiting pathetically to be swallowed up. There was a huge crowd of onlookers, most of them silent but some cheering. My companions were like small boys: calling out the names of the different regiments, exclaiming at the modern tanks and whistling at the wonderful horses.

I was quiet, fully conscious that I was caught up in a moment of history. Even so, I had no grand emotions. And I certainly had no fear as a British person watching the German army pass within yards of me. What I do remember feeling was more actual and commonplace:

tremendous tiredness and relief at having found somewhere to stay. But as the hours passed and the seemingly unending spectacle continued, I began to feel a little ashamed at having accepted the invitation. I thought of my family and friends back in London and of the fears for the future that they must have. I wanted to go back to the hospital.

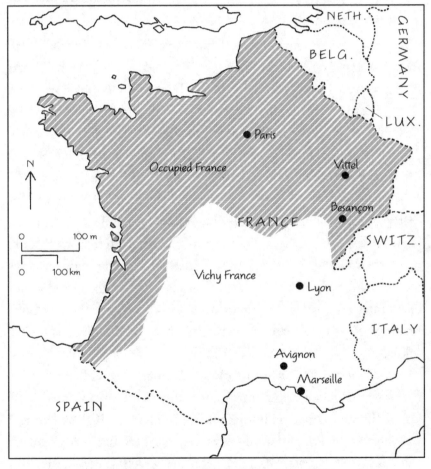

Occupied France and Vichy France from 1940
The Germans took over the Occupied Zone, the richest and most densely populated parts of France. The smaller part of the country – the *zone libre* – was ruled by Prime Minister Pétain from the spa town of Vichy. The demarcation line was heavily manned by German authorities.

The following afternoon I visited the injured British serviceman. I went to the room number I had been given by Mr Close, knocked on the door and cautiously went in. Propped up on the bed sat a young man with his head swathed in bandages. I smiled weakly at him, not knowing what to say. He stared back at me for a while then shouted out.

'Pat! My God! Pat Say! What are you doing here?' He let out a laugh. 'It's me. Ben Everton-Jones.'

I gave a gasp of amazement. Ben was an old boyfriend of my sister's from London. The last time I had seen him had been at a farewell party in Hampstead a couple of nights before I had left London.

He explained what had happened to him and the other men. He was an RAF officer who had been shot down a few days previously. Although his head injuries were horrific, he assured me that they weren't life threatening. The others had been less lucky. One, Major Toby Tailyour, was close to death. The other, Lieutenant Mike Ansell, the British Army's youngest commanding officer, lay blinded. His unit had been cut off in northern France and had taken refuge in the loft of a farm building. Some retreating British soldiers had mistaken them for Germans and had fired on them, hitting Ansell in the face at point-blank range. An American ambulance crew working for the Red Cross had transported the three of them to the hospital disguised as French soldiers.

As I looked at Ben in his bloody bandages I suddenly became overwhelmed. Life was becoming a nightmare. All I had wanted to do was get home to England but it looked like I had got it all so wrong. I was trapped in Paris and would never see my family again. My pent-up fears came to the surface and I began to cry violently. Ben was terribly embarrassed by my outburst but very kind.

'Don't worry, Pat,' he said reassuringly. 'Look, we're both in the system now. They'll send us home as soon as they can.'

He probably thought of me as a burdensome kid sister. I didn't mind. Ben was a link with the normal world back home. After that I saw him whenever I could.

I was to spend just a few weeks at the hospital. They passed quickly. The hours were long: I woke up at 5 a.m. and started swabbing down the corridors half an hour later, with a break in the afternoon while I slept flat out. In the evening I waited on the doctors in their dining room. They were confident and detached Americans and appeared to find the arrival of the German army merely an interesting phenomenon. They were supposed to finish their meal by eleven but would often stay chatting until much later while I worked around them and tried to hurry them up. All the breakfast things would have to be laid before I could run out into the night to my couch. The one compensation was that I could finish any left-over wine or champagne.

I kept a low profile and hardly spoke to anyone during my stay, apart from Ben. There seemed to be no English staff around. The doctors were friendly enough but distant and my French co-workers largely ignored me. Perhaps they were afraid.

I certainly had no feelings of fear, especially as the US Ambassador arrived in the maids' dressing room one day to assure us that we would all be protected, whatever our nationality. I was completely cut off from the outside world and was shielded from the German occupation of the city, cocooned as I was in that big hospital and exhausted by the long hours of work. I was just one of many. As at boarding school, I clung to the comfort of a routine life in an institution. My one outside sortie to watch the Germans entering Paris had been at the beginning of my stay. I had a special permission pass to be out after curfew so I could go the short distance to my flat after work but I hadn't used it to go further afield. Midnight was no time for an English person to be scuttling around the outskirts of occupied Paris.

This rather sheltered life lasted precisely three weeks. One morning early in July I was summoned once again to Mr Close's office. He beckoned me to a chair. There was an uncomfortable silence while he fiddled with his tie and avoided eye contact. His jovial manner of our previous meeting had gone.

'Miss Say,' he said at last. 'I'm afraid you'll have to leave immediately. The German authorities have asked us if there are any English people here. We shall have to tell them the truth. It would be awkward for all concerned if you were caught here. Not least for you, of course.'

'But you told me I'd be looked after!' I spluttered in fear and anger. 'So did your ambassador.'

'The British Interests Section at our embassy should be able to do something for you,' he said by way of reply. 'It's a Mr Sutton in charge, I believe. Could you please see Matron immediately to make your arrangements for leaving.'

He looked away as if to end the meeting. 'I'm sorry, Miss Say,' he muttered quietly.

I had never believed his expressions of concern for me. So that was that and thank you, Mr Close.

I left his office and wandered down the long corridor. For the first time since I had left the Manguins at the station in Avignon I was really frightened. I went to the flat and packed my things. The martinet of a matron took my uniform and wished me well with some doubt in her voice. She allowed me to telephone the US Embassy from her office. I was out of luck. Mr Sutton was away until the day after next.

I went to the staff canteen and sat glumly over a cup of coffee. I did not even have anywhere to sleep that night. Whom could I turn to? I had the address of Claude Manguin's sister, Lucile, who ran one of the most notable dress houses in Paris on the rue Gambon but I didn't think I could call on her. I was beginning to realize that I was actually dangerous to people. I was an enemy alien and if a huge organization like the American Hospital felt threatened then I could hardly ask a French businesswoman to help. She might be jeopardizing her livelihood (and perhaps even her personal safety) if she sheltered me. I was completely alone.

I thought of my parents. They must be sick from worrying about me. I had sent them a couple of letters from Paris but I doubted whether they had reached them in the confusion of these past weeks. Hopefully they had received my last letter from Avignon, posted nearly a month before in early June. But even that would scarcely have been of comfort to them: I had written that I was going home via Paris of all places! I sat at the table for what seemed like hours. There were tears in my eyes. The doctor who had taken me to the victory parade came over and asked me what was wrong. I explained my predicament. He listened carefully then squeezed my hand.

'Look, Pat, I'll see what I can do. You hang on here.'

He hurried off. I sat for a long while. The silence was finally broken by a loud, American voice from across the canteen.

'Where is she?'

I looked up to see a formidable sight striding towards me. Here was a thick-set woman of late middle age; raddled, I suppose you might say. A cigar drooped from her lips. She was dressed in an immaculate American Ambulance Corps uniform. She beamed at me and took off her cap to reveal a large head of closely cropped hair. On her wrist she was wearing a bulky, man's watch.

'I'm Hoytie Wiborg. Dr Murray told me all about you. Don't worry, kid, we'll get you out of here.'

She gave me a firm handshake and sat down heavily at my table. She explained rapidly that she was one of a team of drivers allowed by the Germans to bring seriously wounded French prisoners to the American Hospital for treatment. She was full of enthusiasm for my case.

'Why don't we bandage you from head to toe and take you in the ambulance away from Paris? Or you could pretend to be an American and join the unit! Or pose as my daughter.'

I shook my head. I was quite overwhelmed by this barrage of ideas. Even the most ridiculous seemed plausible in that mood of despair.

'I asked the ambulance drivers a few days ago if they could take me. But it's too risky for them.'

'There are loads of things that we can do for you,' she said as she got up. 'Let's go.'

I had no choice but to trust this woman. I followed her in a daze. We drove off in her white ambulance into the centre of Paris. She left me at a cafe and came back a couple of hours later with a wide grin on her face. She had found me work in a police canteen near by. We walked over to see it. She introduced me to the supervisor, bade me a quick farewell and hurried off.

That was the one and only time I was to see Hoytie in Paris. I had been too bewildered by the force of her personality and by the sheer misery of my situation to show any curiosity about her. She had arrived out of the blue to organize my life and then simply disappeared.

It wasn't until I met her again very briefly in Marseille at the beginning of 1942 that I discovered that Mary Hoyt Wiborg was an heiress whose money came from the long-established and distinguished American firm of Wiborg and Ault, 'Makers of Fine Printing and Lithographic Inks'. It was an enlightened firm that had commissioned posters by Toulouse-Lautrec and other painters. Hoytie had lived in France for many years and had been a well-known lesbian in pre-war Parisian artistic circles, socializing with the likes of Stravinsky, Diaghilev, Picasso and Cocteau. She had fallen in love with the formidable arts patron, Polish-born Misia Sert. Hoytie tried unsuccessfully to seduce her in the sleeping compartment of a train to Venice and was content after that to be one of the gang as long as she had a place in Misia's life.

She was accepted as a good-hearted joke by her friends when not too irritating for words. She was a real character who had never fulfilled her ambition of achieving a place in Proust's *Remembrance of Things Past*. In the autumn of 1939 she had opted for war work, doing her bit for the country that had looked after her for so long.

I didn't know any of this at the time, of course. Looking back on her now, she seems like a caricature lesbian, masculine and hard-drinking. But at the time I simply thought that she was a rather fearsome old lady and quite reminiscent of one of my great aunts. She fulfilled her mission to help me that afternoon in July without behaving in any more personal a way to me than that of a caring aunt. I suspect now that she had to give the police canteen a good subsidy to take me. I always remember her with gratitude and affection.

CHAPTER FIVE

The Police Canteen

The police canteen operated from a closed-down primary school on the rue du Bac, a long, winding street in the elegant *7ème arrondissement* just behind the Chamber of Deputies. Such canteens had been installed all over Paris to feed the policemen whose families had left for the countryside to escape the German occupation of the city.

Once again I was swept into a strict routine of work that started early and went on into the night. I lived with the concierge and worked like a slave. I expected no wages but money was not a problem, given that the British Interests Section at the US Embassy allotted me 300 francs a month (about £70 in today's money). I worked a fifteen-hour day, spending long hours at a smelly sink washing up greasy plates. I had two afternoons off per week. The local *commissaire* made sure that the Germans were duly informed of my existence and I signed my name as an enemy alien every day at the *Kommandantur*.

For much of my time at the canteen my main worry was the chef. He was a tall, muscular and fearsome character straight out of a Zola novel who would usually be drunk by noon. He would curse *la sale petite anglaise* who had once again refused to gouge out the eyes and tongues in the calves' heads before they were cooked. He tried to attack me one afternoon when he was particularly drunk. It took two policemen to drag him off, leaving him with a couple of teeth missing and a determined grudge against me.

The real compensation for all this hard work and aggravation was that there was plenty to eat and drink. After all, no one was going to let the police starve. We also received extra supplies of country food sent by the police families who had fled to regions such as Normandy and Brittany. Usually, by seven in the morning I would already have eaten sausage and bread, swilled down with red wine. I would sit down to meat and vegetables piled high on my plate at three in the afternoon (when the last of the police were back on duty) and again at about midnight.

The canteen quickly divided into pro-German and pro-English groups. The latter were certainly more numerous, perhaps reflecting the fact that the police were treated by their new German masters as a necessary labour force of degenerates and were under strict military discipline. Many bridled with resentment at this state of affairs and every day someone would have a new story of German insolence.

There were fierce arguments and even fights. The pro-German police would curse the English as I served them at the table, repeating propaganda stories from Dunkirk: how the English had refused to let the French get into the boats and had bayoneted them in the water. Everyone was predicting victory for their own side. One particularly obnoxious policeman goaded me relentlessly for a few days with the 'news' of a successful German landing at Dover and the taking of hostages.

Over the summer I got to know the *Septième* well. But (as at the hospital) I had neither the time nor the inclination to go further afield. The little I knew of what was happening in the outside world came mainly from the rumours brought to the canteen. This was perhaps why I got so easily rattled by the pro-German police. They knew of my worry about my family in England and loved goading *la sale petite anglaise*.

Now that I was based in the centre of Paris I saw on the walls the propaganda posters aimed against the British: John Bull the killer; Churchill as a menacing octopus, his tentacles crushing screaming victims; and one showing a drowning sailor holding a French flag with the caption 'Remember Oran'. This last poster totally perplexed me at first, given my lack of information or news about the war, until someone explained that the British had sunk most of the French navy at Oran in North Africa, so as to prevent it from falling into German hands. It didn't take long for some of the police at the canteen to start complaining loudly at how the Royal Navy had murdered hundreds of French sailors.

The Place de la Concorde was bannered with bright yellow instructions and directions signed by the German Kommandant of Paris. The civilian population (unlike the police) generally found their conquerors to be courteous and correct in those early months. German soldiers were allowed to gorge themselves on chocolate and butter, take local girls out to dances and wander round the city calling out 'Spazierengehen, Fräulein?' in the hope of getting a date. It was all very disturbing to me, to say the least. At night, in the concierge's little spare room, I would hear the drunken singing of songs such as 'Wir Fliegen nach England' from the bar below.

One of the policemen at the canteen gave me a bicycle that had been left behind in the exodus. Naturally it had a crossbar and was so large that I could not put both my feet on the ground when I wanted to stop. As in Avignon, I became a source of great amusement to those who watched from the cafe tables as I struggled to control this massive machine. Luckily there was little traffic. Even the Champs-Elysées was often deserted, as few people had permits for private cars. I soon learnt which of the police on duty on the roads were anti-English, as they were the ones who made me wait at the empty crossroads so that I toppled off my bike!

I had two male protectors that summer. One was Mr Edward Sutton, the Deputy British Consul who was in charge of the British Interests Section at the US Embassy. I met him when I went to the embassy after I had been at the canteen for a few days. Perhaps I am being unfair, but it seems that Mr Sutton was one of the very few British consular officials who did not pack up and run as soon as the sound of German guns approached. He was a hardworking man from Guildford, in his early forties and with his thinning hair carefully drawn across his scalp. His face seemed to have a perpetual look of worry. Maybe this resulted from his being continually shouted and screamed at by irate English people who could not believe that the brave words 'without let or hindrance' on their passports did not, in reality, mean much.

As I sat in his office for the first time, he chided me gently for not having notified him immediately upon leaving the American Hospital. He also took over the responsibility of allotting me my small monthly allowance of 300 francs.

'Now, what about your parents?' he said in his quiet, measured way. He looked down at the paper on his desk. 'Commander and Mrs Say. I don't suppose that you've managed to contact them?'

'I've written to them a couple of times but I've no idea if the letters have got through.'

'Probably not,' he said with a resigned smile.

'I was rather hoping you could help me.'

'Of course. Try and get something to me tomorrow if you can.'

As I returned to the canteen for my evening shift, I realized that I was hiding from this mild-mannered official the desperate concern that I felt for my family in London. I had recently witnessed the chaotic fall of Paris and was convinced that London was about to experience a similar fate.

My real worries on this point show up clearly in my first letter home from the American Hospital. Amazingly, my parents received it many months after it had been sent. Written just days after I had witnessed the German army entering Paris, its tone is quite breathless, almost hysterical:

It is just sheer bad luck that I should have got everything fixed and arranged on the very day that I should have kept away from Paris – I got in like a lamb . . . if only I can feel that you . . . above all are making arrangements in case of emergency to get out . . . do believe me that you will be in a terrible position without a car . . . I must feel that you will not stay in such imminent danger. I wouldn't try and write to me. I think of you all practically without ceasing and have learnt to be brave . . . please get somewhere as safe as possible . . . remember go quickly or it will be impossible. My love – my love – Baba.

The day after my first meeting with Mr Sutton, I arrived back at his office with a letter in a similar vein. It would have both terrified and alarmed my poor parents if it had ever reached them, particularly at that time when Britain seemed to be on the brink of invasion. Mr Sutton read my words, paused thoughtfully and began to make amendments with a pencil.

'Try to sound confident, Miss Say,' he advised. 'Not frightened. Your parents would not get much relief if they received this letter.'

'But aren't the Germans going to attack us any day? Look how quickly France collapsed. Won't we go the same way? I want my parents to leave London now!'

I looked at him imploringly. I was near to tears and almost hysterical with fear. Apart from Ben in the hospital, Mr Sutton was the only English person that I had had a conversation with since the German army had arrived in Paris a month before. I had been subjected to a barrage of victorious German propaganda over the previous few weeks and found it difficult to believe that England could hold out for long against the expected German onslaught.

'We can only hope for the best,' he said quietly, handing me his draft. 'Look, try something along the lines I've suggested here. You may use the room next door. But please hurry. I need to get this off by noon.'

I went into the little room beside his office and wrote a much jollier letter. In it I lied that the people at the canteen were 'extremely kind' and exaggerated somewhat that the concierge looked after me as though I were her daughter. I reassured my family that having got myself into this mess I had landed on my feet and was in no danger. I ended:

> Have confidence in me above all — this is a wonderful experience and I am in no danger. I may be home any time, any day — you won't worry any more will you? God keep you safely dearest M and Pappa ... remember I have good, influential friends and will not run any risks.

I kept up this brisk, almost matter-of-fact tone in the next letter that I was able to send in early August via Mr Sutton. I even claimed that this sudden change of existence was doing me a lot of good. I was in the safest possible spot, I wrote: 'I shall probably come home bristling with efficiency!'

Mr Sutton took a fatherly interest in me. On my afternoons off I would go with him to Chantilly, to the Bois de Boulogne or in a *bateau mouche* along the Seine. We seemed to talk mainly about how to get out of Paris. One day I went to meet him at the embassy to be told that he was no longer there. I discovered that he had gone with the first batch of British men to an internment camp in Germany. I never saw him again.

My other male protector that summer was a policeman at the canteen called André Boinet. He was a tall, good-looking young man who had recently got married. He was very pro-English and saw to it that I was protected from the numerous hostile policemen who patronized the place.

On a couple of occasions André took me to drink coffee with friends of his at the Paris Mosque near the Botanical Gardens. This was a wonderful treat: the total peace and quiet inside the lovely building, the beauty of the colours, the breath of an ancient civilization not yet in chaos. All this calmed and soothed me. I remember sitting with him on the steps leading to the Tuileries Gardens one hot afternoon, watching the horses of the little roundabout going quietly round with no children to ride them. I did not feel isolated or alone when André was near. He helped me to settle down to my canteen life without bothering too much about the outside world.

Yet even in the most determined isolation the outside world has a strange way of impinging. One memorable afternoon I was finishing lunch in a deserted canteen when André came in looking very worried.

'Mam'zelle Rose,' he whispered.

'What is it? There's no one here, you can speak up.' I immediately began to panic.

'I have something to ask you. Some old friends of mine have been hiding two English soldiers in their home. They have fed them and given them French clothes to make their getaway. My friends are frightened now. The soldiers have stayed too long. They should leave before anyone notices. Could you speak to them?'

'Of course', I said. 'Give me a few minutes to clear things away.'

We drove in silence in his police car to the south of Paris. I was worried. Of course, I wanted to help André who had been so good to me over these past few weeks. But for the first time I was coming into contact with people on the run. If we were caught the consequences could be severe. A decree had recently gone out that anyone found harbouring British nationals without registering their names at the local police station would be *en peine de mort*.

We arrived at the small house. The elderly owners ushered us silently up to the attic where the soldiers were hidden. I received a shock. In front of me were two vast Scotsmen fast asleep in their makeshift beds, with empty wine bottles, dirty plates and playing cards strewn over the floor. They were complete with sporrans and kilts. One of them had flaming red hair. It was as if they had come straight from a casting agency looking for stereotypical Scotsmen! I burst out laughing, much to the surprise and annoyance of André and his friends.

'I'm sorry,' I said, quickly stifling my amusement. 'But I don't see how they could possibly pass for Frenchmen. They could hardly pass for Englishmen.'

We woke up the two slumbering giants. Their accents were difficult even for me to decipher, so goodness knows how the elderly couple had coped. After some time I came to understand that they were prepared to make their way to the Pyrenees and over into Spain if I would accompany them.

'We canna make it on our own, missie,' said the red-headed one. 'Ye ken the language here.'

'I can't possibly go with you,' I replied. 'I'm registered with the German *Kommandatur* as a British citizen and I have to sign in every day.'

'Och, so yer's a spy,' he said in disgust and spat on the floor in front of me.

André took a step forward. For a fleeting moment I had a horrible vision of him trying to tackle the two of them single-handed.

'Now look here,' I informed them haughtily. 'You are endangering the lives of these good people who are sheltering you. If you are caught, you'll be put in a POW camp. But they won't be so lucky. They'll probably be shot. The same goes for me.'

André translated this to his friends who nodded vigorously in agreement.

'Anyway,' I continued. 'It's your duty as soldiers to make your way back to your regiment at all costs. You simply have to clear off.' My prissy impersonation of a schoolmistress seemed to do the trick. They weren't deserters, they were just biding their time a while.

André informed me a few days later that they had left that very night. When I eventually got back to Britain I made some enquiries and found out that they had indeed managed to get home (complete with kilts and sporran). They had even been decorated for devotion to duty.

At the end of August, when the concierge at the canteen fell ill, I moved temporarily to the Young Women's Christian Association by the Champs-Elysées. A few Englishwomen were staying at the hostel but my long hours of work meant I had virtually no contact with them. Very early each morning I walked across the Pont de la Concorde, past the Chamber of Deputies and along the Boulevard Saint-Germain to the canteen. We were now past the heat of midsummer and the mornings were often misty. These walks were wonderfully peaceful.

As the summer progressed, Parisians began to trickle back to the capital with terrible stories of the exodus: bombing on the roads, starvation, families separated, children lost and similar horrors. For most of them it would probably have been better to have stayed put in the first place. But the government had, after all, fled Paris just before the Germans' arrival and the collaborationists had made things worse by encouraging people to flee. The herd instinct had simply taken over.

The atmosphere in the city changed as the months went by. Those who were Jewish or who had no papers began to hide as best they could. The increasing lack of food and a raging black market dominated many people's thoughts. Propaganda was rife and false rumours circulated by the hour. One report that persisted for a number of days at the height of the Battle of Britain was that Churchill had been replaced as Prime Minister by Lord Halifax, who was suing for peace. Ridiculous to imagine now perhaps, but it is difficult for anyone who has not experienced it at first hand to understand the insidious power of propaganda and rumour after weeks of hearing practically nothing else.

As we came into September it became obvious that my time at the police canteen was drawing to an end. Each day the number of policemen there dwindled as their families began to return home. There was less and less work for me, especially at the evening meal. One morning a police friend took me to one side. He told me that the English lady in charge of the YWCA (where I was still staying) had been arrested, apparently for listening to the BBC. He warned me that my days at the canteen and at the YWCA were numbered. I had to move on.

But what was I to do? I had no idea how to leave Paris. I was told that it would cost several thousand francs (perhaps over £1,000 in today's money) to cross the demarcation line into the *zone libre*. I simply did not have that sort of money. There was always the prospect of going to Hoytie Wiborg for more help, but I had no idea where she had gone. One policeman told me he had seen her. 'C'est un homme,' he giggled maliciously. Anyway, I didn't want to push my luck with her.

Once again, I was seriously worried for my own safety. So much for the blithe assurance to my parents that I was in no danger! It was obvious that I would have to look around for somewhere else to live and work. I couldn't run the risk of staying on at the YWCA, which seemed to be increasingly exposed to random checks and arrests.

What I really wanted was some way of staying in Paris unnoticed until something turned up and I knew what to do. In retrospect, this may seem unadventurous but to my mind it was sensible. I had watched the agony of panic flight. Enough was enough for the time being. I would bide my time in Paris, even though it was occupied by the Germans. I thought it was safer than other places, especially London.

The dilemma over my future was to be solved quite by chance. One day in late September a very distinguished-looking lady arrived at the canteen asking for me by name. Without introducing herself she came straight to the point.

'Would you like to come and look after my children? I can offer you accommodation. We live near by at 98 rue de Varennes.'

I said yes immediately. I couldn't believe my luck.

That evening I took my things over the few blocks to the big, two-floor flat where Madame Georges Izard lived with her family of four children all under the age of ten: Michèle, Madeleine, Marie-Claire, and the youngest child, Christophe. The flat was in a beautifully elegant, eighteenth-century building in a very smart part of town. My room looked down across the narrow street into the garden of the Rodin Museum.

Madame Izard told me that she had heard about my predicament from a policeman friend of hers. I suspected Hoytie Wiborg's hand here but I never asked and was never told. Our arrangement was mutually convenient: now that she had found someone to look after her children she could set about looking for her husband, Georges. He had been arrested immediately after the German occupation and she was worried that he would soon be transported to a German POW camp.

Maître Georges Izard, *avocat à la cour* (barrister), was already a well-known personality in France. Born in the south of the country and the son of a primary school head teacher, he was one of the youngest Deputies in parliament when elected on a socialist ticket in 1930. He had had an outstanding career at the French Bar, dividing his interests between politics, journalism and the law. I was not to meet him until after the war, when I found him to be a quiet, saintly man with a welcome sense of humour.

Madame Izard, by contrast, came from an aristocratic Norman family of generals and cardinals (her brother, Cardinal Danielou, was in the 1970s rumoured to be a candidate for Pope but died scandalously *in flagrante*). She was tall and slim, with an aquiline nose. She was always elegantly dressed and seemed to have an unlimited variety of fur hats and coats. On the third finger of her right hand was the largest diamond ring I have ever seen. I was in awe of her for the short time that I knew her in 1940. She seemed a somewhat distant figure who gave the impression that she expected to be obeyed. She was very kind to me but it was understood that I was under her roof as an employee. It was not until after the war that I got to know her well and came to value her as a friend.

She soon left Paris to search for her husband and was away for a number of weeks. I was quite content to look after the children while the grumpy loyal housekeeper Jeanne ran the home. During the week I was free for most of the day, apart from taking the girls on the Métro to and from school in Neuilly where their grandmother, a well known educationalist called Madame Danielou, ran an exclusive *pensionnat* (boarding school) for girls.

The rue de Varennes was a long street full of government ministries and smart offices. We were just a few doors away from the magnificent Invalides military museum, which I passed daily on my way to register at the *Kommandantur*. Perhaps ironically for an English person, I used to take comfort in the knowledge that Napoleon's tomb was housed there. It seemed to symbolize a greatness and defiance in France that was, at this time, lost.

I would take three-year-old Christophe on the daily trips to register my presence with the German authorities. In his formal suit he looked for all the world a bright English boy. His contribution to the war effort was a cheeky 'Good Morning!' to any German soldiers he encountered on our walks. Luckily, I think this greeting was received as 'Guten Morgen' and so passed unnoticed! We often walked around the quiet streets of the *Septième* with its bright swastika flags waving from the government buildings. For some reason, this sight affected me more than the forest of German signs and notices around the Place de la Concorde. It was a troubling sign of permanence to see such elegant streets taken over by the occupying forces.

Those months in the latter half of 1940 were a difficult and strange time for Parisians. No one was sure what was going on: prisoners were being shipped to Germany and people were in hiding everywhere.

Although it was still too early for organized resistance, a few spoke confidentially to me of the magic letters BBC and RAF.

Madame Izard took me to see some notable friends of hers. Misia Sert, for example, had a splendid apartment on the rue de Rivoli. She had been at the centre of the pre-war Parisian cultural scene and been feted by Renoir and Toulouse-Lautrec (not forgetting that she had also been the object of Hoytie Wiborg's unrequited love). Nevertheless, I thought her rather dumpy and undistinguished in comparison with Madame Izard. One day I was taken to see old Madame Ritz tucked away in a small room at the top of the Ritz Hotel, where Coco Chanel and her German officer lover later stayed. Madame Ritz was very gracious. I don't remember why we went. Perhaps she needed help, being Jewish.

I got a small glimpse of what it meant to be Jewish in Paris at this time when one evening I met a rather frightened, middle-aged woman called Ginette Seidmann at the Izards' apartment. She arrived when Madame Izard was out and we chatted for a while. She told me that she was originally from Golders Green in North London, very near to where I had been brought up. She was married to a French doctor, Paul-Émile, and had lived for many years in France. As Jews they were already on the run. She stayed a long time that evening, most of it closeted away with Madame Izard in hushed discussion.

Her war story is told with great verve in her memoirs. She and her husband hid all over France, sometimes outwitting the Germans by just a few hours. Ginette relates in her book how, later in the war when the Izards were making a temporary home near Bourges on the Loire, Madame Izard sent her a postcard saying: 'This is where we are living. Take the train and come and stay.' They were hidden there and looked after for many months. She marvelled that the fervently Catholic Izards should risk their lives and those of their four children by sheltering two Jews. After the war Ginette became a powerful figure in Paris as a director of the Balmain couture house, where she was very grand indeed. I saw her once again from afar in London in the 1950s. She was busy attending to Marlene Dietrich.

Madame Izard showed much patience and kindness (and also courage) in taking me into her house in the first place. Not all her friends approved: Serge Lifar, already busy directing a ballet at the Opéra, asked that the English girl wait outside when we went to visit him. In retrospect, I can't blame those Parisians I met who felt that they had enough troubles and difficulties of their own without getting mixed up with an English person. Many did not feel this way, of course, but I remembered how different the behaviour of the bistro patron had been when I asked him to look after my luggage on my arrival in Paris from just a few days later when I went to fetch it.

I was still anxious for word of my parents. I had now been in Paris for three months and had not heard from them. Had they received any of my letters? I learnt much later they had been officially informed early in August that I was registered with the US Embassy in Paris. My father had since then been making desperate and unsuccessful attempts to get in touch with me, including trying to contact HMG's Trading with the Enemy Branch at the Treasury. But, of course, I didn't know this at the time and desperately searched for ways to get news through to them.

An opportunity to do this seemed to present itself one morning when I was on my way to the *Kommandantur*. I met an old friend from the police canteen called Laurent. He was a senior police officer from the Toulouse area in the *zone libre* who was in Paris on a regular basis. He was a tall, fleshy man with a mane of carefully combed black hair and a luxuriant moustache. He had always been very friendly to me and extremely pro-English. We had often chatted at length at the canteen. He would show me pictures of a surprisingly stern-looking wife and three adorable young children.

When I met him that morning I told him about my concerns for my family. He thought for a moment and asked me if I could meet him later that day. I agreed. We went to a small, below-stairs bar very near the Louvre. It seemed to be full of off-duty policemen. I finally plucked up the courage to ask him what had been on my mind since I had met him that morning.

'Monsieur, I wrote a letter to my parents but I can't send it from here. Could you possibly post it for me from Toulouse?'

Laurent shook his head sadly.

'An officer in my position could not commit such an illegal act. I would be aiding an enemy alien of the Third Reich. The consequences for me and my family could be extremely serious.'

'Of course. I'm sorry I asked.'

'But I could write to your parents myself. There is nothing illegal in that. I could inform them that you are registered here in Paris and are well.' He gave me a rich smile. I nodded slowly, as I began to understand the situation.

'Alors, does that suit you, Mam'zelle Rose?'

Yes, it suited me. The price, of course, was that I was to go to bed with him. We both honoured the arrangement. We walked to a brothel very near the canteen and made love in a small room surrounded entirely by mirrors. I still have the letter he wrote, along with a rough translation in my father's hand. It was written on headed paper from the Hotel Terminus-Galilée in Toulouse and couched in a flowing, French provincial style. 'Monsieur le Commandant, les malheureuses circonstances de la guerre,' it began. 'The unfortunate circumstances of the war do not permit your daughter Rose Mary to communicate with you [. . .] She is in good health and is employed as a governess.'

Now that I felt more settled in Paris I looked up Claude Manguin's sister, Lucile. The workroom of her thriving dress house was going full blast. Who were the women buying the expensive clothes? I wondered to myself as she showed me around. But I didn't ask. I had learned to keep my mouth shut about the survival tactics of those I knew. Lucile's affairs were managed adroitly by her husband André, who was a chuckling, jovial chap. They were extremely friendly towards me during my stay, taking me for drinks at the elegant Les Deux Magots on the Boulevard Saint-Germain and to dinner at Foyot's (a great treat) where we ate wild strawberries. I visited them at their elegant apartment on the quai de Béthune, where the walls were hung with paintings by Cézanne, Renoir and, of course, Père Manguin.

My life was generally smooth and comfortable that autumn in Paris. I had managed to let my parents know that I was safe. By now I considered myself part of the Izard family, part of the *quartier*, where they were very well known and respected. I was 'plus française que les françaises' and indeed felt more in sympathy with the conquered French nation than with my own people. Understandable, perhaps, given that I had no regular news from Britain.

Christmas was not far away. I no longer thought about a knock on the door.

PART TWO

Enemy Alien

DECEMBER 1940 – MAY 1941

CHAPTER SIX

Arrest and Imprisonment

*O*ne morning in early December, as I was hurrying the girls along to get them off to school, Madame Izard arrived in the breakfast room. She was accompanied by three policemen.

'Rosemary, these gentlemen wish to speak to you for a minute.' There was a slight note of concern in her voice.

I nodded to the three men; I recognized them from the canteen where I had often served them. I was still feeling the after-effects of a late session with Lucile Manguin and her husband the previous night. The men stood there for a few moments looking quite hesitant. Then the tall, plump one (Paul, I thought his name was) stepped forward sheepishly.

'Mam'zelle Rose, we would like you to accompany us to the *mairie*. It's only a routine check-up for a short while. But you will need to bring a bag of your things with you,' he added quickly.

The children were startled and frightened by the policemen. They held on to me and began to cry. I soothed them and told them that I'd be back by the time they returned from school. Jeanne and Madame Izard helped me to put together some things in a small bag. I said goodbye to the family and stepped outside with the men, who were apologizing profusely for having to take me.

'The car is down the road,' the tall one told me awkwardly. 'Would you like a cup of coffee at the bar on the corner?'

I would. As we sipped our coffee they told me they were acting under German orders.

'But I'm registered. My papers are fine,' I protested. 'This is just a check up, isn't it?'

'Wait and see, Mam'zelle Rose.'

'For what? A new German order?'

'Maybe.'

That they were obviously very uncomfortable with the whole situation didn't register with me, even at that stage. I thought they were simply embarrassed by the children's noise or by the fact that I knew them. I certainly wasn't frightened and didn't take any of this seriously. It was probably yet another piece of German bureaucracy. These polite men couldn't be a threat. After all, I had often seen them eating and joking with their friends. There might be some other English people at the station and I could then find out what was happening.

'Au revoir, Mam'zelle Rose . . . Ayez courage,' they all wished me when we got to the *mairie*.

The building was packed and noisy. A crowd of women were waiting around, all laden down with bags and possessions. I joined them. A few more came in as the morning wore on. We all chatted, wondering just what was going on. Most of them seemed to be English. There were numerous French policemen and German soldiers all busily checking and stamping various papers and passports. They looked very focused. I began to realize that the situation was more serious than I had first thought. At one point the rumour went round that we were to be imprisoned in a camp in Germany. The police told us nothing. I doubt if they knew anyway.

I recognized one of the policemen from the canteen who had been friendly towards me and I asked him if he would deliver a note to Madame Izard. I scribbled it in pencil on a scrap of paper. Amazingly it has survived. In translation it went:

I am writing you a quick note – we are still waiting at the Commissariat. There are about thirty old Englishwomen but the morale is magnificent. I think I shall be interned for at least the winter. There is talk of our being taken near Tours. In the end nobody knows anything. I thank you for all your kindness. See you soon. Rosemary.

In the afternoon we were piled into black police vans and driven fast across Paris. I could see little out of the high-barred windows to tell where we were going but I guessed it would be to one of the train stations.

We were unloaded at the Gare de l'Est. The scene that confronted me was quite awesome. There were hundreds and hundreds of people. They were mainly women, but also numerous children and some elderly men. I noticed a group of nuns huddled together and some sick or infirm people being helped along. Everyone seemed to be milling about confusedly, clutching their personal possessions. The noise was deafening, with people shouting and protesting. German soldiers were everywhere but they were having a hard job keeping the crowd under control.

After a short period of total confusion we were bundled onto a train. We waited for several hours in the freezing cold, eventually moving off in the dark. As we scrambled to lean out of the windows, some French railwaymen who were working on the tracks waved and called out, 'Bonne chance, bonne chance.'

My journey to imprisonment had begun. I felt curiously detached and calm. I understood, of course, that the situation was grave: we were almost certainly going to be imprisoned somewhere as enemy aliens. Yet I seemed to have no feelings and no reactions. How could I be afraid when I was surrounded by so many people in a worse state than me?

The journey was to last for two days. Conditions on board the train were horrendous. There were no toilets or running water. The compartments were unlit and unheated in that bitterly cold winter.

There was a constant noise of crying and high-pitched wailing. With all the self-absorption of youth, however, I couldn't appreciate the great misery and suffering around me for the infirm, the sick, those with young children and the elderly. In my carriage there was a lady who must have been at least eighty. She was almost totally blind. Another was bedridden. Looking back on it now, I dread to think what they must have gone through during those two days. Later I learnt that a couple of babies were actually born on the train and that a poor, three-day-old child had died on the journey, his mother having been taken from her bed at the maternity hospital.

On and on we travelled, being shunted into sidings for hours at a time. Occasionally we stopped briefly at unknown stations and were given thin soup or sausage meat and bread by German nurses. We were desperate for water. I read later in an account by a nun that her group so longed for something to drink that they refreshed themselves with eau de cologne until a little old Nazareth nun managed to spill the lot. The stop-overs were frantic affairs, as we all scrambled to get some food or water before the train pulled away.

After two days the lavatory situation was unimaginable. We managed as best we could at any stop when we were allowed down beside the tracks. It was an extraordinary sight to see women of all sorts and ages openly relieving themselves in front of the guards. In between the stops we had to use our compartment as a toilet; the stench by the end was overwhelming. I was told later of one resourceful lady who used her toilet bag as a container, with the contents being emptied out of the window.

Who were all these women and why had we been carted off in this way? My initial impression of the huge crowd at the Gare de l'Est had been that we were an incredible mixture of people. I was right. But all of us had one thing in common: somewhere, at some time, in some way, we all had the word 'British' stamped on our papers. Purely because of this fact we were now prisoners; a reprisal, the rumour went, for the British Government having incarcerated enemy aliens on the Isle of Man earlier in the year.

Many of the people on the train had quite tenuous links to Britain. In those days a woman took her husband's nationality and his name would be on the passport. This meant that there were bewildered French widows on the train who had married Tommies in the First World War. They spoke hardly a word of English and had no desire to lose their French identity. I talked to a couple of women who were fishwives from Arcachon, where they sold their fish in baskets at the quayside. Long ago they had had brief marriages to English soldiers, who had since died or returned to England. A number of women had English husbands who had simply left France at the beginning of the war, thinking that their French wives and children would be safe. There were White Russians with so-called Nansen passports.[3] There were Jewish women from Palestine, a British Mandated Territory at the time. There were also women from all parts of the Commonwealth, including some Afrikaners who were deeply unsympathetic to Britain. In all, there must have been some thirty-odd nationalities among us.

Some of the women were – like me – 'proper' English, for want of a better phrase. That is, born of English parents and with an English home, but in France for various reasons. There were the Bluebell Girls, dancers from the Folies Bergère (traditionally English), girls who looked after the horses at the Longchamps racecourse, women in fur coats and leopard-skin hats straight out of a P.G. Wodehouse novel, middle-aged governesses or nannies and prostitutes from the French Channel ports

---

[3] The brainchild of the Norwegion explorer Fridtjof Nansen, these were internationally recognized identity cards given initially to refugees from Russia fleeing the Bolshevik Revolution. They were issued under the auspices of the League of Nations by various countries, in this case the United Kingdom.

and the *maisons closes*. There were many quite elderly women who had lived in France for years, some since before the First World War. They had survived that war unscathed and many were bewildered by their arrest. We 'proper' English probably made up less than a quarter of the total. I didn't realize at the time how protected that made me. I was told later that even in the allocation of seats on the train we were given preferential treatment. I don't know if this was true.

In my compartment there was a young English girl with blonde hair tightly curled into a bun. She was one of the most typical examples of a prefect at an English girls' public school that I had ever set eyes on. I looked at her superb self-possession and slightly questioning manner towards me with complete understanding. As the train lumbered through the Parisian suburbs we regarded each other blankly for a while and then smiled with open relief.

'How long have you been in Paris?' she asked.

'A few months.'

'Did you come over with your parents or to see friends?'

'I was working in the South of France and was advised to go home via Paris.'

It seems bizarre to think now that we were sitting on that train delicately finding out each other's social position. But then nothing had actually happened yet to jolt us out of ourselves. We had seen the Germans in Paris and had not been hurt. And unlike most of the passengers, we were already away from home.

A young girl with black, curly hair was crouched in the corner watching us. She had been crying and seemed very young and frightened. This was my first sight of Shulamith Przepiorka, or Shula, as she was known. She wrote to me after the war:

When we got to the train I looked for young people among all these poor, old, grey, frightened women. I saw you, Pat, with your curly hair and your unmistakeable English manner. You were talking to another very English girl and I didn't understand a word. Then you said hello to me and started talking in French, which gave me back my nerve. I hoped we would stick together.

Shula told us that she was the daughter of a Jewish leather worker and an immigrant Polish woman living in Porte Saint-Martin. She was born in Haifa during a family visit to Jerusalem, then in Palestine, where a British official had registered her birth. She thereby had a British passport unlike the rest of her family. She spoke no English and was desperately worried about her relatives.

We stopped for a long time at Belfort, very near the Swiss and German borders. Rumours had gone round that we were going to work in a munitions factory near Hamburg or that we were being sent to a prison camp somewhere in Germany. I suppose this was the unspoken fear of us all; if we could somehow stay in France we would be safe. But there was no definite news. The German guards in the corridors refused to tell us anything when we finally got going again.

'We're changing direction,' someone called out excitedly. 'We're going south.'

'We're headed for Besançon,' a bossy woman in the carriage told us. 'It's an old garrison town near Switzerland. It can't possibly be our destination. There's nothing there.'

But it was at Besançon that we stopped. It was almost worth it just to see that woman's face. It was a scene of utter chaos as we spilled out onto the platform after our two-day ordeal, shuffling and cursing as we gathered our belongings together. A reception committee of German officers and guards awaited us. They did not have the same smooth, self-satisfied manner we had got to know among the occupying forces in Paris. These soldiers seemed flustered and disorganized. Our official reception involved lots of roll calls, shouting, dogs barking and waiting around for what seemed like ages. It was all unpleasant and frightening. After such a long and uncomfortable journey we were in a state of shock, exhausted and famished. And the cold! It was early December and we were in the foothills of the Jura Mountains.

Eventually we set off. In front of me were the nuns in their traditional headgear of great, white cornettes wrapped over stiff hats. I counted five different religious orders on that walk. We climbed a steep road, watched by sullen, blank-faced inhabitants. We discovered later that they thought we were a consignment of British spies. Perhaps they could see nothing but trouble ahead. We passed the remains of old medieval walls. The town below to our left was wonderfully picturesque. It was enclosed by a river and several hills, each one topped with what looked to be an old fortress.

Finally we approached huge, grey barracks. As we shuffled through the entrance gates we saw the sentries in full battledress, with rifles at the ready. The barracks, in traditional Napoleonic style, were made up of three huge blocks of four-storey buildings on two sides of a large, cinder-covered courtyard that was at least the size of a football pitch. There were outhouses and offices at the far end of the yard, thereby enclosing them on three sides. A further set of buildings on our left extended the barracks. On each corner of the yard there was a primitive lavatory open to the sky. The buildings were bleak and surrounded by a high brick wall that was festooned with barbed wire.

As at the town station, our reception from the German soldiers here was one of confusion and much waiting around. I was surprised to see a number of male prisoners at work in the camp. It was not until later that we heard how Besançon had been a last-minute choice for us. The Caserne Vauban barracks had until the previous day been occupied by thousands of British and French male prisoners of war who had been captured before they could reach the beaches of Dunkirk.[4] Dysentery had broken out in the stifling heat and dirt of that summer tragedy. Most had been marched away to Germany the day before we arrived but a hundred or so French prisoners had been kept behind to clean up these Augean stables. They had hurled buckets of water around the rooms and down the stone steps, burned infected rubbish and generally attempted to restore some degree of order to the place. They were just finishing when we got there but they had left behind them an indescribable mess.

The luggage carts appeared and spilled out our things into the snow. There was a rush for them, which was halted by an impeccable English officer who stood barring the way. He was very suave and self-confident and looked just like the screen heart-throb of the day, Leslie Howard.

'Now ladies,' he shouted above the melee. 'I want you to line up in three groups. Those under thirty on the right, those over fifty on the left and the rest of you in the middle here.'

He had a clear, commanding voice that could easily reach across a crowd of several hundred women. He also had an officious NCO who went around repeating the officer's instructions and trying to prod us into action. Unfortunately, most of the women didn't understand much English and those who did took no notice. A male prisoner started to translate the instructions into French but even he didn't seem to have much grasp of English. The confusion worsened as women milled about the courtyard trying to keep an eye on their belongings while being pushed and shoved into three groups. Eventually we were sorted. I wasn't much interested in the proceedings as I only had the small bag that I was carrying.

---

⁴ The Marquis of Vauban, an adviser to Louis XIV in the seventeenth century, was one of the greatest military engineers of all time. He upgraded or constructed hundreds of fortresses in France, a number of which are now UNESCO World Heritage sites.

Each group was (with much relief) allowed to collect its possessions. We were then marched across to our block, Bâtiment A. Some French male prisoners, true to form, attached themselves to our younger age group. They led the way. 'Wait and see how clean your room is!' one of them shouted gleefully.

We were led up a steep, stone staircase. At each floor I could see long, dark, narrow corridors with rooms going off at either side. Reaching the fourth floor, I walked into Room 101, my future home. I stood there, dazed and dismayed. We were in a room about the size of a small hospital ward. Straw palliasses and army-issue blankets were strewn about on the stone-flagged floor, which was swimming in filthy water. A wood-burning stove stood in the middle of the room. Over the walls were the numerous marks of swatted bugs and insects. There was an overpowering stench of urine. The wooden bed frames had been piled down at the far end of the room, where there was a vast hole in the ceiling.

The other girls looked equally aghast. My stupefaction lasted only a few moments before all my boarding school training came to the surface; it had at least taught me to look after myself.

'Come on,' I said to Shula. 'Let's get our bedding sorted then we can go and see what else they've given us.'

We rooted around to find the least damp straw mattress and blankets and dragged the bed frames near the stove. Hearing a commotion in the courtyard, we ran outside and over to the far end where a crowd was gathered. We both drew back in shock. Women were already fighting to grab anything from the pile of sorry equipment left over by the previous occupants. They were watched with amusement by the sentries. We looked on in horror for a few minutes. Then a middle-aged woman near me marched up to a sentry and poked him in the chest with her index finger.

'Can't you do anything about helping us clean up this place?' she shouted. She sounded Canadian.

Rosie in Welsh Girls' School uniform in 1927.

Rosie (right) and her sister Joan on a Girl Guides trip to Germany, 1935.

Farewell at Victoria Station: Rosie (second from left) with her mother, father, boyfriend Bobby and brother David.

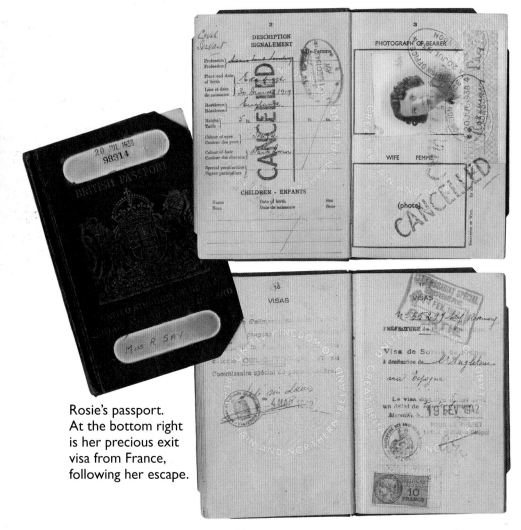

Rosie's passport.
At the bottom right
is her precious exit
visa from France,
following her escape.

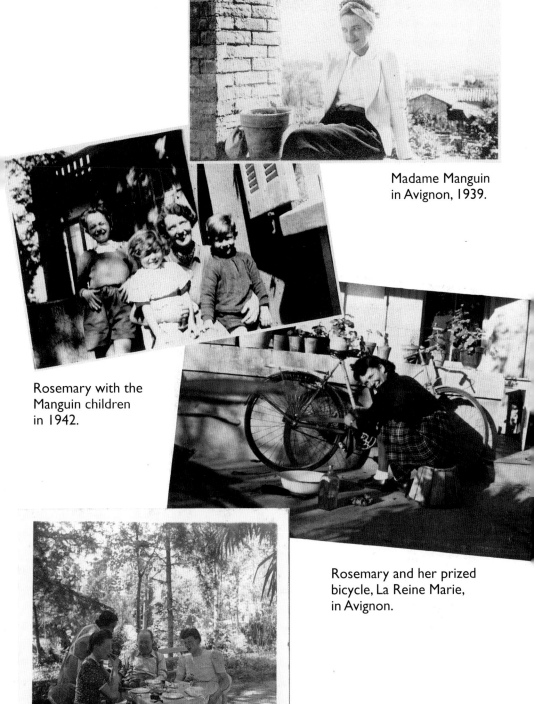

Madame Manguin
in Avignon, 1939.

Rosemary with the
Manguin children
in 1942.

Rosemary and her prized
bicycle, La Reine Marie,
in Avignon.

The Manguins and Rosie
in St-Tropez.

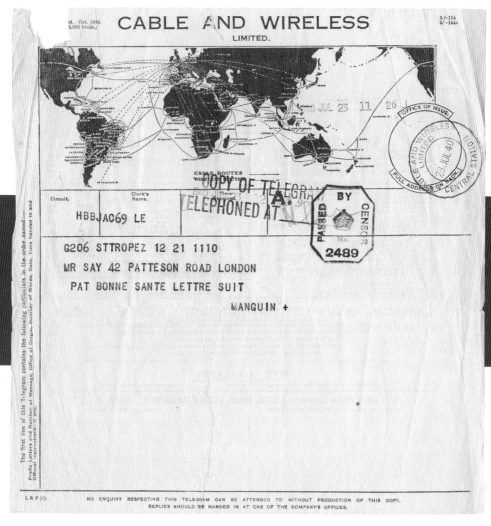

Rosie is in good health: a cable from Claude Manguin to Commander Say, July 1940. By then, France had fallen.

Madame Izard and the children.

Je vous écris un mot en vitesse – on attend toujours au Commissariat – il y en a une très faible d'Anglaises, mais le monde est magnifique...

Je crois que je suis internée pour l'hiver au moins – au pire de vous enverra à côté de Tours.

Enfin, on ne sait rien – Je vous remercie bien pour votre gentillesse – à bientôt

Rosemarie

Note scribbled in pencil at the police station to Madame Izard on Rosie's arrest in Paris, 1940. It was delivered by a friendly policeman.

Rosemary's German registration papers, Paris, 1940. At this time she was working in a police canteen and had to report to the *Kommandantur* every day.

Der Chef des Militärverwaltungsbezirks Paris

- Verwaltungsstab -

Bescheinigung.

Über angeordnete Meldung britischer Staatsangehörigen.

Frau . I z a r d . Cathérine . . . .

wohnhaft . 98 . Rue de .Varenne. . . . .

hat heute folgende britischen staatsangehörigen gemeldet:

1.   S a y Rose Mary

2.

3.

4.

5.

6.

Paris, den 16. Oktober 1940 . . . .

Für den Chef des Militärverwaltungsbezirks Paris

Der Chef des Verwaltungsstabes

Im Auftrag

Imprisonment: the barracks at Besançon, originally built in the Napoleonic era.

Roast chicken, plum pudding, sweets and champagne: Rosie's imaginative birthday menu drawn by Shula in Besançon, 1941.

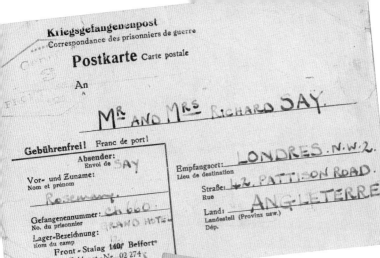

German offical postcard for POWs, sent from the Grand Hotel, Vittel, to Rosie's parents.

'Plenty to do': Rosie reassures her anxious parents and asks them to contact Frida's.

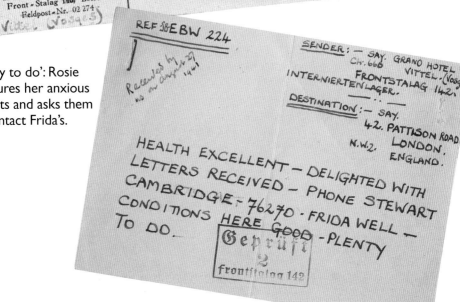

Part of the escape route: in the foreground a soldier keeps watch at the main gates and to the left stands the guardroom.

Surrounded by barbed wire: imprisoned in Vittel. The collection of hotels contained in parkland made a very effective prison.

(Mémorial de la Shoah/CDJC)

(Left) Fellow inmate, Shula Przepiorka, daughter of a Jewish leather worker and imprisoned because of her British passport.

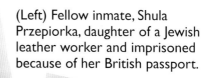

Fellow escapee and great friend Frida Stewart.

Inside the Grand Hotel in Vittel: (from left to right) Frida, Rosie, Shula and Penelope.

The soldier looked at her in astonishment and growing fury. Then he fired three shots rapidly in the air. His superior officer came rushing up for an explanation.

'He's telling the officer that the woman was laughing at him,' a stout lady translated for us. The woman was quickly bundled away by her companions.

We both grabbed a spoon and a bowl and quickly went back to our room where we found that our group was beginning to sort itself out. It was a good couple of hours before a French prisoner barged in to tell us with a smirk on his face that dinner was served. I went back down to the courtyard to queue for soup, ladled out from vast urns by German soldiers with aprons over their uniforms. The portions were tiny and I asked for more. The soldier responded by spitting into my bowl with great accuracy.

As dinner came to an end there was a sudden commotion among the Germans. A white-haired man had arrived with a smartly dressed woman and a small child. He was theatrically attired and wore a wide, black hat. The Germans seemed deferential and rapidly escorted his party away. I never saw him again. I was told later that this was Edward Gordon Craig, the son of the famous Victorian actress Ellen Terry and a distinguished figure in the theatre himself. Apparently, he was sent back to Paris soon after this where he spent the rest of the war.

Most people were desperate to wash away the dirt after that long train journey. The facilities were bleak, as we soon discovered: the bathhouse was out of use and some rooms had a single cold tap and a stone basin. We had nothing. Like many others, we had to make do with the large horse troughs in the communal washroom on the ground floor of our building. On that freezing evening there was pandemonium and something approaching panic as hundreds of women tried to attend to their own toilet. The few lavatories at the corners of the courtyard were totally exposed. They did nothing to answer the needs of such a large number of internees, many of whom were elderly and infirm. I turned away as I saw two nuns approach the open latrine. I couldn't bear to witness their humiliation.

I could not even attend to my own meagre toilet. I had already made the devastating discovery on the train that I had forgotten to pack my sponge bag at the Izards' flat. As I lay on my mattress that first evening, with the raw December wind coming in through the hole in the ceiling, I was totally preoccupied by the fact that I didn't have a toothbrush. I had no idea how or when I would get another. It was as if I couldn't or wouldn't believe the whole horrendous situation. So my mind focused obsessively on this one small thing.

My forgetfulness certainly affected me deeply in the months and years to come. I think sponge bags must be the luggage equivalent of handbags, full of treasures that only you know the reason for: the jar of cream with the last bit at the bottom that you are saving or the special flannel which has the rough corner to rub away any dry skin. I know that ever since this oversight I have found packing totally stressful, even for a short weekend away. And it was to be my toothbrush (or lack of it) that would become the centre of my screaming nightmares when I finally got home to London. For a long time after my return I would have the same dream: I had returned to the POW camp from which I had escaped and would be asking the German sentry if I could just go back in to make sure that my toothbrush was there!

Before I went to sleep that night it finally struck me that I was now a registered prisoner. With the perversity of human nature I had already memorized my new address: Chambre 101, Section 8, Bloc 2, Bâtiment A, Frontstalag 142, Zivil Internierunslager, Caserne Vauban, Besançon, Doubs, France.

CHAPTER SEVEN

Settling Into Besançon

*H*undreds more prisoners arrived during the weeks that followed. There must have been nearly four thousand of us by Christmas. Every inch of space, including the cellars, was used as accommodation.

We counted ourselves lucky in our room. The huge hole in the ceiling at the far end meant that there were only eleven beds, even though the room was easily big enough to fit perhaps thirty. We were all young. I was installed between Shula and Christine, my new friends from the train journey. There were eight other occupants: a Mauritian girl called Rosemary whose husband was to be tortured by the Gestapo; Olga Scrieber, who was big, blonde and good-natured; Penelope Brierly, an English art teacher living in Paris who was very left wing; Margaret Heaton, an elegant English sculptress; a mother and her very small daughter who would sit for hours without saying a word; a pregnant Austrian girl who was soon to be released; and a devastatingly attractive Parisian called Marie.

It is often the most belligerent or the most self-sufficient people who cope best in prison. This was certainly the case at Besançon. Christine and I had fewer problems than many of the others in adjusting to life there. Our education at English boarding schools was to serve us well after all!

Each room had to select a *chef de chambre*, who would liaise with the German authorities. I proposed our ideal prefect-type, Christine, who was unanimously elected.

'First off, we need to put together a rota for collecting food,' she said as we huddled around the stove. 'It's daft for us all to go down individually and queue. Especially in this weather – we're all freezing. Let's choose two people who can collect each day and they can bring the soup to the rest of us.'

Queuing for food meant standing for perhaps an hour in the freezing cold. Each room was given a large, galvanized bucket to carry the soup. When full this was hard work: it would take two people to carry it across the muddy and often snowy courtyard then up four flights of icy stairs. Our hands were so blue and numb after queuing in the cold that we could hardly hold the bucket. The food was inadequate, dirty and monotonous. At midday we would get a meal of beans, swedes or potatoes stewed in greasy water and served from massive copper pots. The vegetables were often rotten or had been sprayed with sulphur. Sometimes there was an odd piece of tough, stringy meat. In the evenings we were given a spoonful of beetroot jam or ersatz cheese (a lurid and tasteless product squeezed out of a tube) to go with our bread. Diarrhoea and food poisoning were common.

Every three or four days we had to queue up to get the bread for our room. The ration was two kilos a week per person of the flat, round loaves. Two of us would take a blanket to a special store behind one of the blocks. When it was your turn you would walk up to the window and hold open the blanket to catch the bread that was thrown out. We were lucky being fit and young, as we could usually catch it before it landed in the mud. The bread was often green with mould. The date stamped on the bottom would usually show that it was at least one or two weeks old and it could only be cut with an army knife. It was made from some sort of rye flour and tasted very sour but not unpleasant to me. Most people found that it upset their digestion and a great many were made ill.

Christine had the job of waiting in line for the fuel chits. These could be exchanged for logs and coal to keep our old stove going. We soon discovered, however, that no amount of fuel could really warm the room. The winter of 1940–1 was one of the coldest in living memory. Even in the rooms that didn't have a large hole in the ceiling, icicles would form inside the windows at night.

Repairing the hole was our immediate concern. Christine had an ingenious solution: she would get it fixed by the German guards, her accomplice being our beautiful Marie.

'Point out the hole in the ceiling to our guard,' she said to her. 'After that, just simper and smile sweetly.' Marie couldn't understand much English, so Christine helped her by putting on a sickly smile and staring coyly up at the ceiling.

Marie was a great sport and a superb actress. She was also the sort of woman who can look like a model even in a prison camp. Having gesticulated to the guard, she just sat down on a chair by the stove and smiled beatifically. He quickly left and returned a while later with three other soldiers all laden with equipment. I watched from my bed as the four German soldiers tried desperately to repair the roof, while at the same time attempting to impress with their efficiency and asking her to meet them. Marie just sat there smiling. Once the roof was patched so that the rain didn't actually come in, she gracefully got off the chair.

'Je vous remercie,' she said. 'Mais je ne comprend pas l'allemand. Nicht verstehe.' ('I don't understand.') She shrugged her shoulders coquettishly. The men were crestfallen and left. They didn't seem to bear a grudge, however, and still gave her special attention after that.

Christine had the measure of the German *Schwester* (Sister) or nurse who ran the entire floor of rooms under orders from the Kommandant of the camp. Schwester Ruth was the cartoon idea of a typical Nazi, with flaxen plaits under her cap and dressed in a grey uniform with a white collar. She was determined to make us drill for her each morning, to leave our beds in military order and to obey instructions at once.

We were equally determined not to jump to her orders. We soon found out she was frightened of the Kommandant, who would bang on his desk with his fist and shout at her, accusing her of making trouble. After one of her more ridiculous orders, Christine threatened to report her alleged persecution to the Kommandant. Schwester Ruth rapidly backed down and together we agreed a truce.

The washing facilities in the camp remained very limited, especially during our first few weeks. The bathhouse stayed out of use until after Christmas and the horse troughs in the washroom downstairs were usually full of ice. We did our best to heat pans of water on the stove in our room. But in that cold winter it was difficult to carry up enough water for cleaning yourself and washing your clothes. Water that was spilt on the steps and in the corridors would soon turn to ice, making any passage treacherous. A basic obstacle to keeping ourselves clean was that we had no soap or towels until the arrival of parcels in the New Year. One fortunate side effect of the shock of being imprisoned was that my periods stopped for many months. I wasn't alone in this. Nearly everyone in my room experienced the same bodily reaction. Thank goodness!

Fleas, lice and other crawlies seemed to be everywhere, from the walls to the mattresses. I was totally obsessed with my own personal bug battle. It was a struggle I would never win but it dominated my life. I wrote to Madame Izard shortly after my arrival that I was terrified to go to sleep at night because of the bugs.

Everyone had a problem with bugs to a certain degree but to some of us victims it became a kind of purgatory. Each of us dealt with them in different ways. Some people scratched while others picked the little devils delicately off their blankets. Shula would take delight in hitting them with her shoe. I tore my skin to pieces. Our Schwester was unmoved. 'Our soldiers have to face far worse,' she said unhelpfully to me after I had yet again begged for help.

I did find a certain relief in the camp infirmary where the St Vincent de Paul nursing nuns in their swan-like white bonnets would delouse us and give out partially effective anti-lice treatment. It only worked until I went back into the dormitory and lay down on the bed. At which point it was as if all the crawlies would let out a great cry of joy, invite their friends round and start to get in some extra rations. My skin was permanently red and uncomfortable. This obsession with lice was to last long after my imprisonment. One day after the war I found myself asking a surprised shop assistant at Selfridges department store in London if the material I had chosen was free of vermin!

Hot showers finally arrived just after Christmas. One morning there was an announcement over the camp tannoy that they were now available in the bathhouse. Within minutes there was a mad rush of women all determined to be at the front of the queue for the dozen or so showers available. I was there with Shula. More and more people arrived as the news spread and the crowd got increasingly impatient. There was lots of shoving and even some scuffles. Several elderly women were knocked down in the crush. The German guards hovered menacingly but seemed at a loss as to what to do when faced with several hundred desperate women armed with towels and toilet bags.

'Now, dear lady, just tell me your name. Madam, could you wait there. You'll get your turn. Madam! Please!'

The haughty, Slavic voice rang out above the confusion. I turned to see a striking, dark woman a few feet away from me taking down names on a piece of paper and shouting out instructions to us. Amazingly, she got the manic crowd under control in very little time. Most of us had showers that day.

I had often seen this woman from afar around the camp but had no idea who she was. Word rapidly went around that she was a Russian princess called Sofka Skipworth who was married to an RAF pilot. She took it upon herself to organize the shower rota for the whole camp from that day on. It was hard work but it had its definite perks, as I discovered years later when I read her autobiography. The two French POW shower stokers were 'trusties' and so were allowed to go into the town. They would come back with steak, wine and other black-market delicacies. They were great characters, especially Marcel from Provence, who had a real eye for the ladies and who could hardly believe his luck. Sofka and her female helpers were also well supplied with hot water before and after the regular bathers had had their turn. At the time I didn't know about Sofka's bathing kingdom or I would have been rooting for the perks like a shot! The bathhouse was the cleanest and warmest place in the camp, even if it was inadequate to cope with the number of women. The water was often turned off after a few minutes – this always seemed to happen when my head was full of soap – or only a few scalding taps would be working. At best we had a couple of showers a month.

It was at this time that a serious bout of dysentery hit the camp. Dirt was probably the main reason for the outbreak, as well as our filthy and meagre diet. Each floor had a single, hole-in-the-ground style toilet but most of these quickly got blocked and were closed. The only toilets available were the open ones in blocks of five at the four corners of the courtyard. There were twenty for nearly four thousand inmates. Dangerously ill women would have to struggle to reach them at all times of the day or night. I remember Christine and I helping an old lady from our landing down four flights of stairs several times over a couple of nights. She was exhausted, dehydrated and freezing.

Some improvements were made to the toilets as a result of the dysentery outbreak. A new set of latrines was built by the French male prisoners. First, they dug a trench. On top of this they fitted a few planks on which rough seat constructions were built, separated by half partitions. The whole thing was roofed. The open trench below the seats was full of excrement, which often overflowed and froze in the snow. The stench was disgusting and the place was swarming with rats.

Among the many rumours that constantly sped around the camp was the sad story of the old dear who fell in the trench one night and was found by a French prisoner the next morning. 'What a death!' a nun said to me as we queued for bread. 'We will pray for her.' I never found out whether or not the story was apocryphal but it was still the case that going to the loo that freezing winter was very dangerous for the elderly and ill. Many, many women – perhaps in their hundreds – died from bronchitis, flu or dysentery. The dreadful state of sanitation, living conditions and food all took their toll. I escaped the dysentery but developed bronchitis and lost about a stone in weight that winter.

In the first few weeks there were quite a few men around the camp, apart from the German guards and officials, of course. Of the British men, most were elderly with their wives. But at first there were a number of younger ones – jockeys, barkeepers, teachers and clerks. There was also a motley selection of other nationals, caught in the general round-up of enemy aliens, with several bemused Norwegians, Czechs and Dutchmen who had no idea why they had been arrested and who were soon released. Two Spanish brothers, Miguel and Juan, who were Republican refugees from their country's civil war, worked as cobblers. A hundred or so French POWs were kept on to work in the camp. Four were doctors based at the infirmary. Many of these POWs were specialized workmen serving as plumbers, carpenters, cobblers and mechanics. Some worked in the offices and stables. In those early weeks our contacts with these French prisoners were very easy and unsupervised. They helped us in practical ways, repairing and mending the broken old bits of furniture and utensils we had been given. They were our lifelines to the town and the outside world: from them came news about the war and much needed black-market goods.

They were also the mainstay of our social life. We'd meet up during the first weeks in a makeshift bar called La Cantine. The alcohol was courtesy of the French prisoners, who would buy it in town. It was fun.

Many romances started in the grimy depths of the bar. I suspect that some of these affairs were more for the goodies from the town that the men could offer than for pure love. Still, La Cantine was a diversion from the routine of camp life, with its attendant boredom and endless killing of time.

My own mild romance was not with one of these French workers but with an enormously tall Dutch lawyer called Paul. Arrested in Paris because he looked English, he had been sent to Besançon and was still there after most of the other male prisoners had left. We would sit in the bar not saying a word, given that he spoke no English or French and I spoke no Dutch or German. Much to my chagrin he was soon to leave the camp. I was teased about him because he was so tall – his nickname was Two Metres – but I really missed him when he was released.

For the first few weeks we had little personal contact with the camp authorities. Perhaps this was because we were all in a state of shock and more concerned with trying to adapt to our new lives. But clashes were inevitable. Our first real confrontation with the Kommandant came a few days before Christmas. One of the regular tasks, which everyone hated, was peeling vegetables. One freezing morning a group of us were sitting in the large and draughty outhouse. We had been there for a couple of hours, surrounded by piles of potatoes, carrots and swedes. We were supposed to be peeling them and it was an almost impossible job. They were black with frozen earth and in varying stages of decay. Our hands were frozen. It was difficult to tell if you were peeling earth, vegetable or human skin.

'I've had enough,' I said, jumping up. 'I'm going to see the Kommandant to complain.'

'Now wait,' Christine said, stopping me. She was as practical as ever: 'If you're going to make a fuss then I'm going to hide some of these carrots first. Just what we want for tea, girls. Frozen, raw carrots.

Lovely. Now you'll be able to see all those little bed bugs in the dark, Pat.'

We quickly salted away a large pile of carrots and then struck. We called out to the Schwester that we wanted no more vegetable peeling drill. We sat there doggedly in the outhouse while she pleaded and threatened. In the end she sent for the Kommandant. He was a middle-aged soldier from the Black Forest, a giant of a man who (luckily for us) had been treated well by the French as a prisoner in the last war. He listened thoughtfully to our protests.

We must have looked a very odd sight, sitting there stubbornly on strike. We were wearing outsize army boots, some with no laces, and the light blue, poor quality overcoats worn by the French soldiers in the First World War that we had been issued by the camp authorities. Underneath we had on just about every garment we possessed.

'Someone has to do the vegetable chores,' he said when we had finished. 'My men are busy enough as it is. I shall have a brazier sent over.'

'Two,' said Christine quickly. 'We need two braziers. One for each end.'

The Kommandant looked at her and gave a slight smile, as though indulging a child. He nodded in agreement and went off, speaking quietly to one of the guards as he did. A while later, two braziers were set up, one at each end of the piles of rotting vegetables. We were certainly warmer from then on but the air in the room would get very unpleasant as there was no chimney to let the smoke escape.

We felt triumphant at our half victory. We had been at Besançon for less than a month and considered that this was a vital confrontation. Honour had been saved even though the work was no less demanding. And we had stolen some carrots! We rudely mocked the Schwester and the German guards for a couple of days, ostentatiously warming our hands on the braziers or deliberately wasting time on our chores, silly little things like that. We didn't realize how indulged we had been.

We rarely gained another concession so easily and our next clash with the Kommandant was to be much more sinister.

A few days after our brazier confrontation we decided to make more trouble. There were loudspeakers dotted around the camp playing turgid, German music, which was continually interrupted as orders were blasted out. One morning, a small group of us got together near the Kommandant's office and began to clap and shout: 'We want Mendelssohn. We want Mendelssohn.' Other women quickly joined us and within a few minutes there were perhaps fifty of us chanting the composer's name.

The Kommandant came out of his office with a look of fury on his face. 'You have been chanting Mendelssohn's name,' he said to us quietly. 'You know perfectly well that he cannot be played. He was a Jew.'

'But we have British-born Jews here and we'd like to hear Mendelssohn,' said a small woman who occupied the dormitory next to ours.

'This is not a holiday camp!' the Kommandant suddenly screamed. He had been goaded too far. 'You will do what I and my officers say. I will not have these disturbances. There is much to be done besides listening to the Jew Mendelssohn.' He stormed back into the office.

We felt a tiny frisson of the sort of fear that must have been felt in so many homes in France. We were only in the camp by chance of our passports. How far those documents would carry for the British-born Jews we didn't know. We wisely shut up and dispersed.

That night a blackout was imposed on the camp. It continued throughout our time there and was to leave us shivering and miserable. The Germans had originally felt it was unnecessary to take blackout precautions, reasoning that the RAF would not bomb British women and children. They had therefore taken the opportunity to billet senior officers and strategic bureau staff around the perimeter. They were correct in that the RAF didn't bomb the camp but the problem unforeseen by the Germans was that the Caserne Vauban was a landmark. It was perched by the loop of the Doubs River with the snow-capped Jura Mountains behind it. The RAF were consequently briefed to guide some of their sorties to Germany over this isolated blaze of light in a Europe that was largely blacked out.

Once the Germans had realized their mistake, the Kommandant ordered us to cover every inch of light, although we were given no equipment to do so. We had no curtains and had to make do with any spare bit of material we could find to cover the windows. But for a while we were one window short, so we had to use a blanket as a blackout curtain. It was left to Christine to draw up and enforce the rota that meant that each night someone had to give up one of her precious blankets during that freezing winter.

Perhaps the Kommandant's outburst over the Mendelssohn episode should have been a warning to us that we could not push him too far. For all his amiable exterior he was still a German officer who was answerable for his actions. He had little patience with any activities that overstepped the mark, as we found out over the Christmas and New Year celebrations in the hall.

Christmas came just a couple of weeks after our arrival. I remember that I had pushed the thought of the festivities to the back of my mind, expecting nothing. One evening I was finally able to scrounge a battered old toothbrush from one of the French prisoners. I had by this stage become desperate, lying in bed each night, running my tongue around my goofy, furry teeth and imagining that they were rotting away. He excitedly told me that his compatriots had been given permission to have a celebration and concert on Christmas Eve provided they were finished before midnight mass.

'You will come, Pat?' he said as he handed me the toothbrush. 'And your friends in the room?' I nodded my assent. I had a slight crush on him but I guessed that he had his eye on the beautiful Marie.

We made ourselves as presentable as we could in our large blue overcoats and turned up at the hall on Christmas Eve. I don't know what the others were expecting but to me it was a wonderful shot in the arm. The French had obviously been saving up for ages. It looked like a real Christmas feast. The tables were decked with meat, cheese and wine. There were even cigarettes, courtesy of their Red Cross parcels.

About a hundred of us (mostly French prisoners) sat down to certainly one of the best Christmas meals I have ever had. Afterwards the tables were pushed away and someone set up a gramophone and we started to dance. Numerous gatecrashing internees joined us. The dancing got wilder and wilder as more and more couples took to the floor. A couple of Bluebell Girls even went into their stage routine, kicking their legs and swinging around together in perfect time, much to the delight of the men. As the party wore on, one girl jumped on a chair and gave a resounding rendition of 'It's a Long Way to Tipperary'. When she finished we all stood up and with great solemnity sang 'God Save the King'. Not to be outdone, the French finished the evening with 'La Marseillaise'.

Inevitably, no one took any notice of the time. The doors suddenly opened and a procession of nuns and their congregation tried to enter for mass. For a while there was complete chaos as soldiers, nuns, dancers and worshippers struggled to carry out their own particular form of celebration. Elderly ladies were whirled around the floor by drunken French soldiers and the priest had to fight his way up to the makeshift bandstand. News must have travelled quickly to the Kommandant that a bacchanalian orgy was taking place. He soon arrived with the guards and they quickly cleared the hall of revellers. He said practically nothing but was unamused, to say the least. I imagine that he foresaw some very difficult questions from his superiors over the incident.

The affair of the midnight mass was quickly followed by the legendary party for the Russian New Year on 14 January. Permission was granted for the sixty or so interned White Russian women to celebrate this in the hall. They got together some food and wine and somehow bought several bottles of vodka. The ensuing party could be heard around the camp. Unfortunately, when the Kommandant and his officers turned up to investigate, one of the women threw her arms around him and kissed him soundly on the lips. There followed a horrified silence. The Kommandant turned red and walked out. His guards quickly dispersed the party.

There was no question of his turning a blind eye to this. He had been very lenient at Christmas but this was too much. We were informed the next morning that festivities in the hall would no longer be allowed. Worse was to follow, for he seemed hell-bent on a total purge. One evening not long after, as we were standing around in the courtyard talking, a group of soldiers in full battledress suddenly arrived and ordered us to our rooms. We were amazed. What was going on? We watched as the Kommandant led his troop of men through the stables and outhouses, dragging out dishevelled loving couples and marching them towards the German offices. The next day the French soldiers could be seen at one end of the yard playing boules or football while their girls waved and signalled to them from the other end, separated by a patrolling sentry. From then on our contact with the French prisoners was minimal.

Much to our dismay the authorities also closed down La Cantine as part of this crackdown. Not long after the Russian affair, a woman got paralytically drunk there one evening and was carried out insensible. A group of Germans soldiers were waiting outside with Leica cameras at the ready. Someone must have tipped them off. We found out later that the ensuing photos were published in a German newspaper under the title 'British Woman's Debauchery'.

The place was closed down and reopened a couple of weeks later as a shopping exchange and mart. Food, wine and toiletries were sold

The Barracks Yard, January 1941, by Frida.

at inflated prices. It had a large notice board where all and everything could be bartered: 'Cigarettes Wanted – Warm Jumper in Exchange'; 'Soap Offered in Exchange for Food'. This was perhaps more useful than a bar but certainly a lot less fun.

CHAPTER EIGHT

People, Post, Prayers and Prostitutes

*O*ur first few weeks at Besançon had produced a sense of near-euphoria, or at least of tremendous energy. We had been totally focused on the need to sort out how to survive in this new and hostile environment. But once the energy had dissolved many of us were left depressed; we felt useless. Our sense of isolation increased over the festive period. What were we doing in the foothills of the Jura Mountains in such foul conditions? With (as yet) no means of communication with home?

One particularly low evening Shula suddenly grabbed a branch of wood we had collected for the stove. Brandishing it, she thrust it into the embers until it was glowing then soused it in water. As the smoke poured from it she climbed onto my bed and wrote across the long wall in charcoal: 'Un pour tous et tous pour un.'

How to deal with the nervous energy generated by hours of immobility and apprehension? Already it seemed that we were going to spend the rest of our lives in Besançon. We all used different ways to cope. Shula was left dispirited for several weeks after writing her defiant slogan. Like many others she would curl up on her straw mattress and turn her face away. Margaret, the sculptress, would lie in bed all day devouring every book she or anyone else could lay their hands on. For me, I needed to move: I ran, jumped, played ball and took part in every game that was organized.

As those early weeks passed, rooms and dormitories closed in on their own circle of inmates and it was no longer as easy to make friends. We became very protective of our dormitory, Room 101. It was known as Les Arts et Métiers. I learnt from another woman that we were considered exclusive and unfriendly. We were not, but we were all young, healthy and quite selfish. We were determined to survive.

Many rooms were seriously overcrowded. A friend later told me that Room 13, for example, which should have had eight or ten people at the most, held eighteen women of an average age of probably seventy. There was one child of five there who lived with his mother. He hardly ever went out and used to leap around in desperately high spirits. A great deal of cooking went on over the communal black stoves which were supposed to heat the dormitory. Each old lady liked to cook her mush in her own way. An anti-fresh air league governed the room and it was always stiflingly hot. The windows were only ever opened when the heat and smell got too bad even for the *grand-mères*. Room 13 was also typical of the constant bickering that went on, occasionally breaking out into open warfare. We young women would laughingly refer to such spats as 'The Battle of the Broken Basin' or 'The War of the Lost Teaspoon', but even our mockery became tiresome after a while.

I made two great friends while at Besançon. Shula was one of them. Although she was quite a few years younger than me, in many ways she seemed older. She had been working since the age of twelve to contribute to the family income and those early experiences had made her a committed revolutionary. She had already decided that what she really wanted was to be an artist. She was forever sketching and drawing, using any medium she could get her hands on: charcoal from the stove or pencils exchanged for cigarettes (an unusual transaction at the exchange and mart, as I pointed out to her).

She had a thick bush of curly, black hair which always seemed wild, regardless of how much she combed it. Her features were large: big eyes, a wide mouth and a broad nose. With her Middle-Eastern appearance and total lack of English she looked even more out of place than most. As a Jewish person she had been saved from a deadlier camp by a chance of fate. Having been born in Palestine, she was the only member of her family to have a British passport. When she was released from imprisonment in 1944 she was to discover that the only other close relative alive was her small sister, who had spent the war hiding in a cupboard and emerged permanently deformed.

My other great friend was Frida Stewart. One evening in January she arrived at our dormitory with her friend Ronka, one of the very few black women who were interned. Ronka came from Nigeria and the two presented a wonderful contrast: Ronka was tall, beautiful, haughty and silent; Frida was short, incredibly thin, with large, bony English features. She was earnest and voluble. That first day she came straight to the point.

'We need to find a new place. We can't stay in our room any more. It's driving us mad.'

I knew that they were in the terrible Room 13 but stayed silent. Ours was enormous; with the roof properly repaired it could easily have accommodated many more. There were only ten of us, now that the pregnant Austrian girl had been released. Our bunks were all huddled at the near end, this side of the stove and as far away as possible from the hole in the ceiling, which had only been roughly patched up by Marie's helpers. The wind and rain still whistled or dripped their way into the room. Even so, like everyone else in the camp we were becoming very protective of our space. None of us wanted any new faces in our dormitory. It was Christine, as the *chef de chambre*, who took the lead.

'Well, of course, there is room. But it's freezing here, you know. And every few days you have to give up your blanket for the blackout curtain.'

'Oh, that's fine,' said Frida, airily waving aside this objection. 'It'll make a change from our room. It's so stuffy and overcrowded.'

'What about the bugs?' I ventured. 'We're overrun with them.'

'They can't be any worse than in our room.'

I blushed. There was silence. Perhaps it was better to have girls we knew (and more or less of our own age) than to have some old battleaxes imposed on us at any time. But Christine still made one last and rather feeble attempt to forestall them.

'I'm not too sure what the Schwester will say . . .'

'Oh, don't worry about her,' Frida said cheerfully, moving towards the door. 'I'll speak to her and be back to you. Bye.'

Her persistence had paid off. They moved in that evening. We quickly learnt that persistence was one of Frida's main qualities. She was a committed Communist who took the war and the Nazis much more seriously than most of us did. Her arrival brought the wider world to our room. She was determined to find out what was happening and was not content simply to read and then ignore the German propaganda notices we were given. She would argue and probe out information from anyone and everyone. It was she who made us aware of the RAF raids, the fighting in North Africa and the German successes in Greece and the Balkans. Frida would spend hours talking to the guards, trying to gauge what ordinary German people felt about the war. She was an enigma to many inmates and considered by some to be suspect. Why would she insist fiercely one day on blocking any German initiative in the camp yet the next day spend hours in earnest conversation with our captors?

Despite our different political views, I immediately understood and empathized with her. We came from the same English, middle-class world and had some London friends in common. Her father was the Dean of Trinity College at Cambridge University, where my brother had recently finished studying. I didn't need her to tell me why she talked to

116

the German soldiers. She was still in that academic world of enquiry and research. Her political beliefs were such that she felt that to challenge the German soldiers was in itself a political act. Like me, she had been arrested in Paris. She had been studying at the Sorbonne and

Rosie (left) at work in the Kommandant's office, by Frida.

had stayed on to sit her exams even as the Germans were entering the city.

Our real common interest was music. We both played the violin and requested instruments from the Red Cross as soon as their parcels started to arrive. We would challenge each other to faster and faster Scottish reels and duets, half the time playing just to keep warm. This would bring women from nearby rooms knocking on our door and asking us to 'stop that racket'. The noise would intensify with Shula and Ronka dancing or pretending to fence to our music. The bugs would literally be dropping off the ceiling.

The violins were one of the many lifesavers from the Red Cross. Parcels, letters and telegrams all began to arrive once a post office was established early in the New Year. We now had contact with the outside world. The British authorities were notified of our existence with names, details and next-of-kin. The whole of the British bureaucracy rapidly swung into action to include us with the thousands of soldiers caught up in prison camps. I had been so worried about my family. Until the end of January I had no means of contacting them. In fact, my father did learn before Christmas that I had been interned but I didn't, of course, know this at the time.

In the first letter to my parents, dated 30 January 1941, I did as much as possible to reassure them of my well-being. I wrote that I was 'well fed and with lots of friends of my own age'. I did not lack for anything, I continued, given that Madame Izard 'looks after me and sends me anything I need'.

This light-hearted tone, which made the Besançon camp sound almost like a French version of an Enid Blyton school, was to be present in all my letters home. In another I boasted of my superb ski suit sent from Paris by Lucile Manguin 'in which I live all day long'. And in my last letter from Besançon I assured my parents that I was getting lots of food parcels from the Izard family in Paris. This was true, but it was followed by the blatant lie that I had put on at least a stone in weight, given the rich contents of these parcels!

Early in February, after nearly two months of imprisonment, I finally received my first communication from home. It was a Red Cross telegram of precisely nineteen words. After reading this I dashed up to my own private hideout on the roof of one of the camp buildings. Tucked in among the chimney pots, I perched on the steep slates to read and re-read the words:

ALL SAFE AND VERY WELL AT PATTISON. MUMMIE, DADDIE, DAVID JOAN BOBBY SEND LOVE. GOD BLESS YOU DARLING GIRL.

I began to cry quietly for only the third time since leaving Avignon. I was no longer isolated. The feeling that my family was still there at the same address in North London and that we were part of the whole POW machinery was very comforting. My mood could not even be depressed by the German sentry below, who was shouting and threatening to shoot me unless I came down.

The post office was great but it involved endless bureaucracy. Actually getting a letter was sheer luck, depending as it did on where your letter was in the vast pile waiting to be tackled by the German censors. On our side, we were all very clearly informed of the details of postal censorship. Letters had to be kept brief and each one was stamped with the reminder that 'Brevity and Clearness in Writing Will Assure Greater Expedition.' The war could not, of course, be mentioned. I spent long hours trying to think up meanings within meanings to write on the printed POW letterforms. I don't think anyone, least of all my family, ever broke my complicated code. Not that they would have learned much more than that I was well and alive! But it was fun to feel that I had slipped something by the German censor.

It seems most extraordinary looking back, but the whole system of communicating with friends or relatives in enemy or enemy-controlled countries operated through the good offices of Thomas Cook & Son Ltd, which was appointed by the British Government as its intermediary. One condition for letters sent to the camp that I especially liked was the instruction that no reference could be made 'to Thos. Cook & Son, Ltd, or any of their offices'. As if our family and friends would waste their precious few words talking about Thomas Cook!

We knew very little of what was going on in the outside world. Strict censorship meant that even with the postal service working, our knowledge of news from elsewhere was still very scanty. The letters we received gave us very little idea of life in Britain. Some news would be brought in by the French prisoners and doctors who had contact with the town and (in some cases) access to Swiss radio or the BBC. But everything was rather vague and we would speculate endlessly about any rumour.

Our German captors were the only other sources of information about the outside world. They related to us with great relish news of the Blitz over Britain that winter. One particularly nasty guard would taunt us at the daily food queue that our homes had been destroyed and our families killed. Somehow such news didn't seem real: it is difficult to believe that any place you know well is changing while you are away from it. Or perhaps that was simply a defence mechanism in the face of the German taunts.

The arrival of parcels in the New Year meant for me the two lifelines of food and books. The food parcels were crucial to our well-being and survival. The first consignment arrived from the Red Cross in February 1941. It was only after they started that my weight began to stabilize. Canada sent powdered milk and maple syrup while from Australia came corned beef. Food-rationed Britain sent jam, butter, tinned steak and kidney pudding, marmalade and cigarettes. In the little parcels hut Christine and I eagerly opened the first package from Britain. The familiar labels of Crosse & Blackwell, Peek Frean and Cooper's marmalade brought back such strong memories of England and our local grocer's store that tears streamed down our faces. The three German soldiers seemed embarrassed and the sergeant brusquely asked us to leave. Only a few days later did it occur to me that they might have mistaken our tears of nostalgia for those of anger at the number of parcels being pinched for their own family homes.

Book parcels were also terribly important, given that the barracks library only contained musty, old military histories. There was an odd and arbitrary system of censorship towards any books sent to us. There seemed to be no rhyme or reason to what you were allowed to keep and what was confiscated. I requested some specific books from the shelf in my bedroom at home. In the parcel that arrived the censor had refused Palgrave's *Golden Treasury* and D.H. Lawrence's *Poems* yet had accepted Oscar Wilde's *Picture of Dorian Gray*, Henry Miller's *Tropic of Cancer* and even an anthology of Russian poetry! For some reason, Dickens seemed to be regularly banned for most people. Frida had a lot of trouble over a book of Matisse and Renoir reproductions, mainly nudes. The soldiers at the parcels offices made her stand there, furious and embarrassed, while they gloated over what they seemed to think was the last word in pornography. Eventually they handed it over with a smirk and 'Nicht gut, Fräulein' ('Not good, miss').

Friends and family sustained me with their parcels. All were meticulously searched and a couple of times were even requisitioned. The ski suit from Lucile Manguin that I boasted about to my parents was a magnificent, haute couture affair in navy blue, together with matching ski boots. From Madame Izard I received food, books and money. My family in London kept me well stocked. I later found a draft of a letter from home saying that my mother was sending various items

The queue for Red Cross parcels, sketched by Frida.

The overcrowded, constantly bickering Room 13.

including: '... soap, chocolate, toothpowder, old skirts and coat. Let us know if there is anything you want.'

Any sort of prison has a drab routine to it. I settled into mine as the weeks passed. We were woken at 7.30 a.m. and began our daily preoccupation with keeping the stove lit and our room warm. After a breakfast of bread and water we had some time to ourselves to clear up and wash and then it was work for the rest of the morning. Given that I could type and knew shorthand, I applied for a job in the Kommandant's office. It was boring and monotonous stuff, with lots of card indexing and archiving of documents. But at least it was warm and I could try to find out what was going on and get as much of the German news as my limited knowledge of the language would allow me.

The afternoons we had for ourselves. There were numerous exercise classes which were run by an ex-PE teacher nicknamed Stanley (I never learnt her real name). She inspired plenty of volunteers and organized a whole series of matches and tournaments in volleyball, netball, rounders and folk dancing. Her classes dominated the afternoons for me. All my school life I had played tennis and netball. I loved the feeling of being physically strong and fit. I felt better in myself when I had run, stretched and jumped away the depression and grumpiness inside me. I wanted to race around the courtyard and leave the others to their interminable debating about the future of the world. I would drag Frida out into the snowy yard and make her play reels and jigs while we bounced around doing folk dances until her fingers were blue with cold.

In many ways, my daily round resembled that of the institutionalized and old-fashioned boarding school that I had only quite recently left. We had dormitories, orders, announcements, games and chapel. 'Lights out' was at 9 p.m. We were preoccupied with food, giggling, sex, gossip and even outings to the hospital in Besançon for the lucky ones. And there was always, of course, the desire to try to beat the system in any possible way.

Looking back, I think that my school experience literally saved me. The camp was not such a shock to me as it was to many others, as Christine and I had both realized in the first few days. Boarding school had given me a sense of detachment and almost childlike selfishness. I wasn't even particularly bothered by the fact that (as at school) I seemed to have been marked out at an early stage as a troublemaker. Perhaps my part in the protests over the braziers for potato-peeling duties and Mendelssohn's music had been responsible for this. The result was that I was not allowed to go to town to visit the dentist. Even the Hospital Saint-Jacques was out of bounds to me when I had bronchitis; I had to make do instead with a painful *ventouse* (suction device).

Others, however, found the environment of the camp extremely difficult. One lady spent most of the day sitting at the entrance to our block, quietly sobbing. Another committed suicide by jumping out of a window. Shula had always been at the centre of a close-knit family and found the emotional life of the camp very hard. She had to learn in a short space of time and under very trying conditions what I had learned over many years at school: how to be self-sufficient and to find your own physical and emotional private spaces. This need to create some sort of recognizable routine in order to cope with imprisonment was common throughout the camp. The old ladies cooking up their messes of dinner, each in their tightly secluded world of a bunk bed and part of a stove, were recreating their own little kitchens.

Some of the more public-spirited women formed a Prisoners Committee early in 1941. At first this body received a lot of abuse and snide moaning, including from our room. But within a couple of weeks elections were held for membership and after that it was well respected. It did invaluable work in seeing that everyone (and not just the strongest) had a fair turn. It kept in touch with the Kommandant and his two administrative officers, one from the Gestapo. The committee also checked that we all received our official POW allowance of 300 francs a month and often made out IOUs for those who were permanently broke.

Even the prostitutes quickly set up their own network. The round-up of British women had not been confined just to Paris. The whole of the Occupied Zone from St-Malo across to the Swiss frontier had been meticulously combed. Into this net went a shoal of girls from the brothels on the Dieppe coast as well as from the red-light districts of Paris, and with them the brothel-keepers.

The professional and highly organized prostitution system was something the Kommandant totally failed to uncover during his purges. Money was exchanged for favours but cigarettes were more easily accepted. A packet of cigarettes would mean two nights spent in the German quarter. Soldiers from private to officer were bribed. One particular brothel-owner from Boulogne with bright red hair and heavy make-up would sit in the courtyard and sum up the rest of us as we walked by: 'Good legs. Could use her.' Marie Ange, her daughter, would nod quietly in agreement.

Many women took (or returned) to religion to help them cope with their internment. There were hundreds of nuns in the camp. Divided firmly into Catholic and Protestant orders, they stood apart from the rest of us. There was one silent order of nuns and the impact of the camp on them and on some of the other closed orders was terrible. They still wore wonderful medieval cornettes: great white swan-wing constructions placed over a neat wimple wrapped tightly around the head. How they managed to keep these headdresses clean and stiff I never worked out. They would exercise in the cinder-covered courtyard like flocks of birds swooping from one side to the other.

Many of the nuns stood up extremely well to this unaccustomed life. They organized a school for the children, study circles and religious

Nuns of various religious orders, wearing their medieval cornettes,
in a sketch by Frida.

plays. They were a calming influence, giving a sense of security to many people. They were very much the carers of the camp, providing nursing and emotional support. They made many true converts as time went on. I wasn't one of them but I could readily understand the importance for many people of the blessings bestowed by these holy women.

My own upbringing in England had been a formally religious one. Indeed, my brother was at the time a hardworking young Anglican cleric in Croydon, where his baptism of fire had coincided with the heavy bombing of that part of London. I had been taken regularly with my family as a small girl to Holy Trinity Church in Great Portland Street. I could remember more of the long trudge past Regent's Park than the

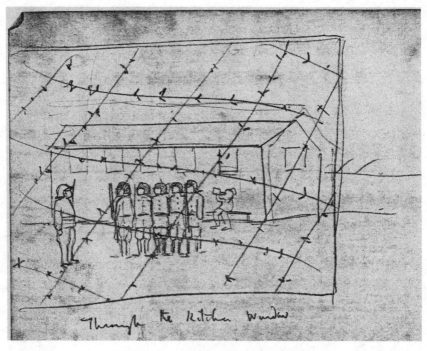

The camp at Besançon, drawn by Frida.

service itself, as I would spend most of the latter under the pew seat trying to read my *Tiger Tim* comic.

Religion itself did not interest me but food did. I quickly discovered that religion could mean extra supplies. The Catholic catechism classes apparently entailed a present of a cake or a biscuit (presumably sent in from the town). I quickly became one of a flock of starry-eyed Catholic novices. It was only when Shula discovered what I was doing and demanded her share that I went too far, even for the nuns. At the end of the next session I went up quietly to the sister and asked if I might have some extra biscuits to sustain me as my friends were too sad to join me in prayer. I was given an extra large piece of cake. But it was accompanied by such a look that I never had the nerve to go back.

CHAPTER NINE

Doctors, Birthday and Moving Camps

*E*ven though I was able to adapt relatively easily to camp life, I still wanted to get out. Indeed, I became increasingly obsessed by this idea as the first months slipped by. Not escaping, mind you, for this seemed to be practically impossible. But just somehow getting out.

I remember sitting on my bunk one day in March writing a letter to Madame Izard in Paris. I was at a very low point, having recently got over a bout of bronchitis. What the hell was I doing here, stuck near the Jura Mountains and surrounded by thousands of women? Especially now that I could see from my fourth-floor window the first signs of spring in the countryside.

In a mean-spirited way, I also felt depressed by the fact that so many women were leaving the camp on a daily basis. Many were British Commonwealth citizens who were being repatriated on the grounds (so I had heard) that their countries had not interned Germans. Ronka, the Nigerian girl from our room, had recently left. Officially the prisoners eligible for release were women over sixty, those with children under sixteen or with husbands over sixty-five. But it seemed that many sick women were being sent home as well. There were about four thousand of us interned in the early days; by the spring perhaps half of these had been released.

I joked in the letter to Madame Izard that the only hope for me in being able to leave Besançon was a chronic illness of some sort that could put me in the next group for release. As I wrote it occurred to me that I might very well be able to engineer just such an illness. I had heard a rumour that soap increased your heartbeat. So why not take an overdose? Would that work? It was worth a try. At least I might get a few days in the infirmary away from the bugs.

The infirmary was staffed by some very suave French POW doctors who had always remained carefully distanced and detached from all of us. They were the heart-throbs of the camp. Much too canny to get into trouble with the Germans by fraternizing openly with the internees, they realized (quite rightly) that it was preferable to be interned in Besançon than in a male POW camp. I had always thought them very big-headed and pompous, fancying themselves in their white coats. Their doctoring seemed to consist of two coloured pills, white and brown, which they handed out indiscriminately. They were, however, the ones who could recommend you being sent to the hospital in town (and thence home) if they really thought you were too ill to stay.

My plan was very crude. For the next week I collected scraps of soap in exchange for cigarettes. One afternoon I dutifully ate my entire secret hoard. Feeling extremely queasy and slightly panicked by what I had done I rushed over to Schwester Ruth.

'I have to see a doctor. I'm ill, really ill.'

She examined me, taking my temperature and pulse, and took me quickly to the camp infirmary. 'This English girl, Rosemary, says she is ill,' she told the doctor on duty.

'I feel dreadful,' I moaned. 'My heart's beating so hard. I want to go home.'

By this time I wasn't faking it. I rushed over to the basin and was violently sick. The doctor gave me what seemed to be a very cursory examination.

'Mmmm. You are the fifth this week', he said quietly, out of earshot of the Schwester. 'The English are a sickly race, no? But very clean!'

I looked at him blankly and said nothing. He gave a slight smile and continued.

'Once a rumour starts in this place, Mademoiselle, it is not just the women who get to hear of it. Luckily it hasn't reached the ears of our Schwester, eh?'

He dismissed me and handed over a small sachet of powder, which he instructed should be dissolved in water and drunk. It made me ill for the rest of the day but by the following morning I had quite literally been purged of all traces of my soap-induced trauma. I was bitterly disappointed at the failure of my plan. I was also a bit shamefaced at having been exposed so easily. I recounted miserably to the rest of the room my total lack of success.

'Pat, you can't seriously have thought it would work,' was Frida's damning comment.

'Why not? I was more worried that it would work too well and I was really going to be ill.' Shula lay giggling in the corner. 'Well, at least we know the doctors are human after all and not pill machines,' I said. 'Let's invite them to the birthday party.'

My twenty-second birthday was on 30 March. I was determined to have a good time. We scrounged a gramophone and some records and bought food and wine from the French prisoners working at the shop. A parcel from Madame Izard provided some special treats. The colourful menu card, beautifully drawn by Shula, boasted untruthfully of roast chicken, plum pudding, sweets and even champagne! Olga did the cooking and entry to our room was by invitation only.

It was a wonderful party. There were about twenty of us. Christine had primed the doctors beforehand on what the drill was to be if we had a visit from the German guards and Schwester Ruth. I would hop into bed and pretend to be ill and they would appear to be looking after me. Putting one over on the authorities was to be the crowning touch to our festivities.

'What is the meaning of this, Doctor?'

The old German sergeant had appeared at the door. He was addressing one of the doctors, who was by now apparently taking my temperature and showing signs of concern.

'We are just on our way into town and I thought we would stop by to check on Mademoiselle Say. She was in the infirmary the other day and we were concerned about her, as you well know.' He looked at the Schwester.

She nodded her head. Authority intimidated her, as we had found in the past, and doctors seemed to possess the air of authority in abundance. He rose from my bedside and made to leave the room.

'Eh bien, Mademoiselle. Perhaps a day or two in bed and you should be feeling fine. Bonsoir.'

And with that the doctors swanned out. The sergeant gruffly told us to keep the noise down and they left too. Amazingly, it had worked! Why I should be an object of concern when the room was full of empty bottles and glasses hadn't seemed to occur to the Germans. The party had been cut short but we were quite happy to clear up. It was the best birthday party I have ever had.

The long, cold winter finally ended a few days after my birthday with a wonderful, warm spell. From my roof perch I watched the snow disappear from the great mountains and the colours of spring push through in the woods below. Margaret, the elegant sculptress, announced one night that with the change in the weather it was time to remind ourselves that we were still part of the female race and dress accordingly.

'Look at you all,' she said. 'You seem to live in old army coats and rags.'

'What about me?' I said in mock outrage.

'Apart from dear Pat, who never seems to leave off her ski ensemble. She's lorded it over the rest of us quite outrageously and for long enough. It's time to change.'

'Hear! Hear!' someone cried.

'I have an idea,' Margaret continued. 'In the little storeroom by the north wing there are a whole load of linen mattress covers. They've been deloused and nobody seems to want them. Let's use them to make some spring clothes.'

We readily agreed. We got dyes of all colours, needles and threads from our loyal group of French prisoners. We bubbled and boiled for two nights and under Margaret's supervision we made skirts, slacks and blouses. They were, in truth, quite basic but we didn't care. We emerged in our hand-dyed and handmade finery feeling like true Parisians. I even left off my ski suit for a while! The change in the weather combined with our new outfits gave us all a new sense of optimism. We had survived the shock of the first few months of imprisonment and the dreadful winter. We felt that we could face whatever came our way.

It was around this time the rumours started that we were all going to be moved to new quarters. By now Frida and I had learned to take such speculation with a pinch of salt. The camp was, after all, a massive rumour mill. The pessimists, who seemed to include most of the Prisoners Committee, claimed that this time we would be moved to Germany, but in our room we were optimistic.

Frida was convinced that the Germans would use us as a propaganda exercise to show the humanity of the Third Reich. Our confidence on this point was somewhat dented one evening when the Schwester arrived after dinner to inform us that our kind guardians were taking us to a lovely new place.

'I cannot tell you where it is,' she said. 'And I shall not be going with you. But I am sure that you will all be very happy there,' she added with a malicious smile.

We were all panicked by this news. The pessimists seemed to have been right: we were being sent to a German camp – the unspoken nightmare for us all. I spent the next couple of days when working at the office trying to get some more information. As it turned out, my concern was misplaced. I got on quite well with the Kommandant's secretary and found out from her that we were going to the town of Vittel, which before the war had been a prosperous watering spa in the Vosges region. Apparently there were smart hotels, a large park, a casino and even bathrooms! I related this news breathlessly to Frida as soon as I could. I thought she'd be pleased but I was wrong.

'So, Pat, that's the end of the struggle,' she said bitterly. 'Welcome to tea parties in the Home Counties.'

'Oh, come off it, Frida. Just about anything would be better than this. It's dreadful here.'

'Maybe it is. But remember that we gain strength only in the face of adversity.'

'That's just a political slogan. For God's sake, Frida, I can't wait to go.' I flounced off with tears in my eyes. I was disappointed by her reaction and dismayed at our argument.

A couple of days later our Schwester told us that we would need to have all our clothes and belongings ready for delousing the following morning. We ourselves were to strip in the showers and be scrubbed down with disinfectant by the Schwesters.

'So, the sedate and bourgeois town of Vittel is frightened that thousands of verminous females will bring an invasion of lice and bugs,' said Frida grimly as the Schwester left the room.

'Well that's understandable,' said Penelope. 'Anyway, I'll be glad to get rid of these dratted lice once and for all.'

This arrangement seemed reasonable enough until we heard later in the day that following our shower we would then have to wrap ourselves in blankets, walk across the cinder courtyard and wait around for our clothes to be deloused. This news did not particularly worry the younger women who hardly gave it a thought. But it created a minor revolution among many of the older inmates. That evening a large

Scottish woman who looked like a retired hospital matron complained bitterly to me.

'It's dangerous to walk straight out of a hot shower into the cold air.'

I nodded vigorously in agreement.

'And what if the blanket falls off or the guards decide to pull one off just for the fun of it?'

'Perhaps we should approach the Committee,' I suggested hesitantly.

'Well, let's see what the others think,' she replied as she walked away. 'But I don't see how that body of wet fish can do anything.'

It turned out the Scottish matron was wrong. There was a great strength of feeling among many of the older women. I'm not sure if it was a result of their fear of being exposed naked in the courtyard or just the anti-fresh air brigade becoming militant but the Committee was persuaded to send a delegation of protest to the Kommandant.

He received us in his office with only his administrative officers present. Fortunately, his Gestapo assistant was away for the day. We argued that the delousing procedure had to be changed: clothes and belongings should be brought to the *douche* and not the other way around. The Kommandant looked concerned. A bevy of protesting females was exactly what he didn't want at this moment. He was obviously under pressure to start the evacuation of the camp as soon as possible.

'Another point, Kommandant,' I added brightly, 'is that you and your fellow officers will surely want your clothes just by the *douche* when your turn comes.'

To his credit, he smiled at this. He seemed ready to reach a compromise. But there was the matter of honour at stake: who was in charge of the camp? He finally agreed to our request but stationed a group of sentries in the middle of the courtyard with rifles at the ready. The delousing went ahead smoothly.

We left Besançon a couple of days later. It was a warm day in early May. What a sight we must have been: thousands of female tramps laden down with all sorts of clothes, bags and other possessions. One woman clutched two saucepans made from cans, while another next to me had three old forks carefully tied up under her belt. It was a very different group from that tired but orthodox-looking collection of women who had arrived a few months before. Our time in Besançon had taught us that even the most despised piece of rubbish could have value.

We trudged in a slow line down the road leading to the railway station. I glanced to the right of me at the town so near by across the river. I could see people huddled in doorways watching us pass. It was somewhat bewildering to be in contact again with the outside world. I had been in captivity since before Christmas.

It took a number of hours for all of us to board the train and even then there was a long delay before we finally began our journey. We had been told to take food that we had saved from our meals: beetroot jam sandwiches and what tasted like dog biscuits, unless you were fortunate enough to have some Red Cross provisions left. Ersatz coffee was passed to us on the train. It was horrible but we still drank it greedily.

I was in a compartment with Frida, six other women and a German guard. He was a thin, middle-aged man with a streaming red nose who came from Freiburg, just across the border. Frida chatted to him. As always she wanted to know about the war and how ordinary Germans felt about it. He became quite friendly and even shared out his scarce ration of chocolate.

Our journey lasted three days and two nights. On and on the train crawled through the dull, flat country west of the Vosges mountains. It would stop for hours, seemingly for no reason and in the middle of nowhere. I have no idea why that journey took so long. It is only about one hundred kilometers as the crow flies between Besançon and Vittel. Over half a century later I did the same trip by car. In the middle of a torrential winter downpour my journey took slightly over two hours.

'I think we're arriving. It's Vittel!'

I awoke on the morning of our third day on the train to hear Frida's excited voice. She was craning out of the window. We all pushed to have a look. Even the guard seemed excited, showing his yellowing teeth through a broad smile. As we slowed down I could make out a number of large hotels that looked boarded up and closed. The train pulled into the station and we poured out.

We marched half a mile or so through the town. As in Besançon, the local inhabitants were out in force and watching us suspiciously. We were told later that this time they thought we were German women staying at the spa for our convalescence. I don't know how this story tallied with our wretched appearance. We passed elegant shops, firmly shut. The whole town had a gloomy and deserted air.

We entered a large, wooded park and reached the entrance of an impressive building, the Grand Hotel. It looked rather like a Parisian apartment block in the *Septième*. There seemed to be a big turnout of German officers to greet us at the entrance. There were also some civilians with cameras. They looked German. Frida grabbed my arm.

'The bastards are filming us! Keep your heads down everyone,' she shouted to those around her.

We quickly realized that the whole scene was being filmed for propaganda purposes, presumably to show how well we were being looked after. So we hid our faces like film stars and all rushed into the building, ignoring the dismayed shouts of the cameramen.

The hotel was in a pretentious, turn-of-the-century style with pillars, gilt mirrors, candelabra and lofty staircases. It was the sort of place that rich patients came to before the war to take the waters. No one then would have imagined that its latest clients would be such a bedraggled collection of women, some encased in mattress cloth and carrying with them all their worldly possessions.

An elderly man in black patent pumps was in the foyer, somewhat frantically trying to organize accommodation for us. He was the proprietor of the hotel, as he told us at frequent intervals. His cries of 'Mesdames, je vous en prie!' seemed to become more fraught by the minute. 'Where is the princess?' I heard him shout.

He smiled ingratiatingly at two rather aristocratic-looking women and led them off to their room. This was presumably one of the better ones on the lower floor which were, I discovered later, as ornate as the hotel: carved marble fireplaces, high ceilings and enormous beds. I disliked the man at once. He reminded me of a pompous restaurant waiter who checks your clothes before deciding on which table to give you. With barely concealed distaste he hurried away a small group of prostitutes down a dark corridor. 'Come this way, Mesdames, this is where you belong,' he said to them.

When he came to us he seemed surprised by our youth. Perhaps he was wondering what damage we could do. 'Room 660,' he said quickly. 'The guard will unlock the door for you.'

My little group of five – Shula, Frida, Penelope, Olga and me – had been given a room on the top floor. We seemed to be in the old servants area, which suited us fine. While we waited for the guard to arrive we clambered up the winding stairs to the roof from where we could survey our new home.

We were duly impressed. Below us were more elegant hotels, including the Palace (which was to become the medical centre) and the Continental (where the older women and the nuns were put). In front of us was a columned arcade of luxury shops all closed and shuttered. Next to this was the Casino with a beautiful dome. We were surrounded on all sides by an enormous park which had a number of buildings dotted about. Everything was closed. The lush, green park and the rolling hills in the distance made it all seem much more gentle, if less dramatic, than the majestic bleakness of the Jura Mountains surrounding the Caserne Vauban.

The guard finally arrived to let us into our room. We bounced on the beds and opened the big wardrobes with cries of delight. There was a bathroom just along the corridor with taps that worked. Luxury indeed!

PART THREE

Breaking Free

MAY – NOVEMBER 1941

CHAPTER TEN

Vittel: The Model Camp

For the second time we seemed to have been moved to our prison camp in a hurry. Food was scarce for a while until the Red Cross and our families caught up with us and the all-important parcels began to arrive. It didn't seem that the authorities had even thought about security, as there were no physical restrictions around the complex of hotels. So, for the first few days we were not allowed out of our building until the German soldiers had installed barricades and barbed wire around the grounds. After that we were able to move about quite freely within the compound, which stretched for a number of acres. But we were not, of course, allowed into the town of Vittel itself.

It would be difficult to imagine two POW camps more dissimilar than Besançon and Vittel. To picture the former, just think of the numerous postwar films about Colditz and the like: dour surroundings, large courtyards, harsh conditions, constant surveillance and the continual presence of lice and other bugs. Vittel, on the other hand, was almost luxurious. We found that there were a number of untended but perfectly adequate tennis courts, albeit without nets. Coming from the bleak, cinder courtyard of Besançon, we were now in the middle of a landscaped park complete with a small pond and swans (this being France, we weren't allowed to walk on the grass). The rules on parcels, food and jewellery were quite relaxed. Most of us had small rooms which we shared with a few others. There were baths on our floor, although the hot water was erratic and limited. Most importantly, there was proper sanitation at last.

We were constantly reminded, however, that this was a gilded cage: it was a prison camp. The hotels had been closed for a year or so and the carpets and curtains remained mothballed. Everywhere was very crowded and noisy; the army boots that many of us had been given at Besançon had wooden soles that created a constant clatter. It was bitterly cold during the first few weeks of that spring until the weather improved. The heating wasn't fired up until the autumn.

It soon became clear to us that Vittel was being used by the Germans as a propaganda camp: a model internment area to show the world that the horror stories and violence attributed to German soldiery were untrue. Hence the newsreel cameras at our arrival. Visiting groups of German VIPs were shown around the spacious grounds and we began to feel like show puppets. One of my friends, Madeleine White, complained many years later that people after the war would dismiss her imprisonment with a shrug, saying, 'Oh, tu étais à Vittel, c'était un paradis.' Yes, it was better than Besançon but as the war went on the nature of the camp changed. It became a staging post for Jews going to death camps in Eastern Europe.

In the early weeks at Besançon there had been a laxity of discipline. Contact with the French prisoners had been easy and frequent. We were able to purchase wine and food through them. It was very different in Vittel. The French male prisoners of war had been moved with us, again to act as general handymen and labourers around the camp. But now they and the French doctors were located in quite separate quarters and we hardly ever saw them.

We also had little contact with the German guards. Indeed, the grounds themselves were so large that we rarely seemed to encounter them. They were ungainly men in their poor quality uniforms, thick dirty boots, all-enveloping helmets and army belts with '*Gott Mit Uns*'

(God With Us) stamped on the buckle. Most of them were very second-rate soldiers; after all, guard duty in a camp such as ours was not for the elite of the army. They lived in an enormous building in the park which we nicknamed the Villa des Fées or Fairies' House.

As at Besançon, Frida managed to spend hours talking to them, trying to find out what ordinary German soldiers thought about the war. Most were imbued with Goebbels's Nazi propaganda and ignorant of everything else. Only occasionally would she come across one who had some glimmerings of doubt and who understood that there might be propaganda on both sides. Such soldiers genuinely did want to hear about life in England.

Like most of the other inmates, I had little to do with the guards. Only a few were approachable. Some had been separated from their families for years and they would sadly show us photographs of young women holding babies. But most were pretty arrogant. When war was declared on the Soviet Union in the summer of 1941, they accepted Hitler's change of policy towards Stalin without question. They were cock-a-hoop and would often goad us by saying that the campaign in the east would be over in a few weeks. Then it will be England's turn, they would add. 'Our Fuhrer knows what he is doing,' was their constant refrain. It was only as the first reports came through of Soviet resistance in the autumn that these men became less enthusiastic about being transferred to the Eastern Front. I was told by Shula after the war that some soldiers would be weeping and drunk as they left for the front.

The Vittel camp was portrayed in a film called *Two Thousand Women*, made towards the end of the war by Frank Launder. It had a star-studded cast that included Phyllis Calvert, Dulcie Gray, Patricia Roc and Flora Robson. The last portrayed an uppity English lady who arrived with a lady's maid; she was to be accused of espionage and sent off to Germany. The first two actresses played the heroines Rosemary and Freda (of course!) It was all pretty silly stuff, with Rosemary at one point sitting up in bed in a negligée to find an RAF man hiding in her room. A discreet love affair starts between them. He evades detection by dressing up in voluminous washerwoman clothes like Toad from *The Wind in the Willows* and finally makes his escape dressed as a German officer.

I watched this film at a cinema in London's West End at the time it opened, when the memory of my imprisonment was vivid and fresh. I found it ridiculous and insulting. I saw it again over a half a century later on afternoon British television. This time I was struck by how well the film portrayed the class divisions that soon appeared. You might see a woman in a hat, white gloves, smart dress and high-heeled shoes chatting to another internee similarly dressed. Yet next to them would be a woman dressed in boots and a First World War army uniform or perhaps a dress made from mattress covers where the dye was already fading in patches. The regular visits of a hairdresser from the town made no difference to me, but to many of the older women it meant elaborate, waved hair and the reappearance of colour. I described the camp in a letter to my sister as a 'mixture of Mayfair with artiness and heartiness'. It was this resurgence of class distinctions that gave our new quarters a sour taste. Bridge parties flourished and those who didn't play would gossip alongside the tables. It might have been any afternoon in Bournemouth! Frida gave a memorable description in a letter home:

> Life's a monotonous but not unpleasant round, a sort of island of rest-curing, reading, tennis, music and it's sometimes difficult to believe that the tempestuous world outside exists . . . There are crowds of bores here . . .

The class divisions were largely as a result of our softer surroundings. There was much more leniency here on parcels. Gone was what seemed the revolutionary boldness shown in those terrible early days of Besançon, when the camp had been severely stricken with dysentery.

Even recently we had shown fighting spirit with the insensitive de-lousing plan. At Vittel, however, we felt almost deflated now that the struggle was apparently over. Although we didn't know it at the time, perhaps we were experiencing the same flat feeling that was to be felt in Britain after the Blitz by those who looked back to that time of camaraderie when everyone had pulled together.

Some of us, nevertheless, still kept up over the coming months a barrage of complaints: over the blatant disappearance of our Red Cross parcels (a constant theme in my letters home), the haphazard censorship of books sent to us and the indifferent quality of the food, even though on this last point Christine and I agreed that it was now just about on par with boarding school fare.

To the dismay of our room, we found that most people seemed to be settling down quite happily for what could be an indefinite period of confinement. They wanted no more trouble. They acquiesced in the break-up of the elected Prisoners Committee and did not query the new appointments made by the Kommandant. He now controlled the unelected British representatives who replaced the Schwesters and who were accountable to him for the smooth running of their particular floors. They all seemed to me to be bossy, middle-aged types. They wore armbands and looked pleased to be helping the authorities (in return, of course, for special privileges). Within a few weeks they had reported on three prisoners who were planning to escape.

We suspected that these women wrote at least some of the unsigned letters that the Kommandant began to receive. Their missives complained of other internees' behaviour. These anonymous writers were the scourges of the place: embittered, jealous and frustrated, they would see themselves as part of a crusade to give the least trouble to the Germans and to hound the rest of us.

With the loss of any community spirit in the camp, I began to look much more not only to my close friends near by but also to my family and friends at home. Like all prisoners of war, I eagerly awaited letters. Red Cross telegrams were often terribly delayed and could say little other than banalities. Yet they provided a wonderfully reassuring lifeline that could be read day after day. Typical was a telegram sent by my father on 18 June:

ALL WELL HERE ANXIOUS TO RECEIVE YOUR NEWS. FONDEST LOVE WE MISS YOU MORE THAN EVER. DADDY AND MUMMY.

My reply to this was (and I can't work out why I was allowed so many words):

DON'T BE ANXIOUS ABOUT ME. VERY WELL AND FLOURISHING. RECEIVE YOUR LETTERS REGULARLY. PLENTY OF NOURISHMENT, MUSIC, TENNIS, FILMS, BOOKS AND RAIN. FONDEST LOVE PAT.

Our families would scrimp and save to send us food, money and clothes at a time when they themselves were cut to the bone. My mother raided my wardrobe at home. I was delighted to find waiting for me one morning a parcel of underwear. At last I could abandon my dirty grey outfit! My parents also sent a large amount of my pre-war poetry collection. Unfortunately this arrived the day before I escaped from the camp and I had to leave it all behind.

Such a lifeline did not exist for all internees. The elderly spinsters who had kept themselves to themselves all their lives, for example, were now cruelly forgotten in the excited morning rush for a precious sign of communication by letter or parcel. We in our high spirits and selfish youth found these women boring and uninteresting.

Their isolation was brought home to me as I sat at lunch one day. A money order from Bobby had arrived. I was in a great mood, discussing with Shula and Olga what we could buy with the money on the camp black market. As usual, food was at the top of my priorities! Succulent dishes were by now being made and sold by many internees and I was determined to have some. It would be better than the dirty-brown soup and the stone-hard bread in front of us. The elderly lady sitting next to me, a Miss Walker, put her bony hand on mine.

'You're blessed to have such good family and friends, Miss Say,' she said simply with a sweet smile.

She was genuinely pleased for me. Yet she was all alone in the world. I knew this because she had told me just a few days before that she had spent her life looking after other people's children as a governess. Not only was she alone in the world but, like many of the older women, she spoke very little French which was the common language of the different nationalities in the camp. I felt ashamed of my self-centredness. I resolved later that day that the least I could do would be to ensure through a friend that some of my possessions went to her if I ever managed to escape.

Money from home could also be used to buy toilet necessities. In the summer a special concession was given to two salesmen who were allowed to distribute toiletries and sewing things. They came every couple of weeks and dashed all over the place scattering talcum powder, soap, flannels and sanitary towels in their wake. Of course, most of these articles were of the ersatz version; toothpaste, for example, seemed to come from a lump of mushed fish gills. We didn't mind. Anyway, it was pleasant to chat to this pair of active little men, especially as we missed the company of the French doctors and the male prisoners. It was also an opportunity to glean some information about the outside world.

I was preoccupied by the need for a spare toothbrush. The old one that I had managed to procure at Besançon was becoming very threadbare. I had asked my parents repeatedly for a replacement but for some reason nothing had arrived. Perhaps it had been sent but had been pilfered before it reached me. I asked one of the salesmen if he could get me one. On his next visit he told me that he had some in his supplies box at the back of the hotel. I went with him along the corridor to choose one.

'In here, Mademoiselle,' he said, opening the door of a small storeroom.

He almost pulled me in, switched on the light and shut the door behind him. Wordlessly he began to fumble with my breasts and made a feeble attempt to kiss me on the mouth. I was revolted by his teeth, cracked and covered with tartar, and turned my face away. He pushed me against the sharp prickles of the upturned brooms and brushes. Just then we heard someone whistling in the corridor outside. He looked at me in apprehension, perhaps fearing that I might scream. Once he was sure that I wasn't going to, he opened the door, ran his hand over his bald head and gave me a toothbrush from his pocket.

'I might have other things for you the next time I'm here,' he said and gave me a conspiratorial smile. 'If we have a bit more time, of course,' he whispered.

'Yes,' I replied feebly. 'Thank you.'

I made my way back to my room. I was a bit shocked by what had happened but at least I had my toothbrush. And in return for nothing! Not as yet, anyway.

CHAPTER ELEVEN

Camp Routine

*A*s in the previous camp, I worked during the week-day mornings in the Kommandant's office. Along with all the non-German office staff, I was now under a taciturn, middle-aged French corporal called Didier, who would obsessively pick his nose when he thought I wasn't looking. I got to know the Kommandant and his officers quite well over these months. Perhaps their friendliness had something to do with the fact that they were confident that Germany was about to win the war and that our countries would reach a peace deal.

One day in early October the news came that Moscow was apparently about to fall to the German army. The Kommandant paced the outer office excitedly as I sorted out some files.

'Fräulein Say,' he said to me in his deep, agitated voice. 'We have defeated Slav Communism. Why should we Teutonic people continue to fight each other?'

'I think, Herr Kommandant,' I replied calmly, 'that the British Government went to war for a cause it believed in. It still wants to achieve its aims.'

'But surely Herr Churchill will now see the futility of continuing the war? He will want to make peace. Your father is a naval man, I know. He would certainly agree that our countries should be friends.'

'I think you would have to ask him yourself, Herr Kommandant, but his answer would probably be no.'

It was the familiar argument that I had with the German officers throughout the summer. As always, my position seemed to puzzle them. They simply could not understand why Britain wanted to be at war with another Teutonic nation. My replies always needed to be carefully couched and to express as little as possible of any controversial opinion of my own. I was, after all, in the Kommandant's office. He was a genial and engaging man but he was not to be trusted and my words could at any time be reported to the Gestapo officer. He, like many of the Germans, had the idea that Britain was a good country but rotten to the core.

Our daily and weekly routines were very ordered. Once I had completed my morning work the rest of the day was my own until 7 p.m., when all the internees were locked in their buildings for the night. I was at the camp from May until November 1941 and for much of that time the weather was wonderful. Stanley, who had been a great organizer of team games at Besançon, continued to set up matches and tournaments using the tennis courts and the spacious grounds. Frida received two new tennis rackets from home and a small group of us would spend endless hours playing, watched carefully and enthusiastically by the German officers.

In the autumn, Stanley had the courage to highjack a visiting Red Cross delegation with a complaint about the regular filching by the guards of our Red Cross parcels. As soon as the delegation had left she was promptly sent away to Germany and we never saw her again.

Reading was the other mainstay of the afternoons. I read for hours up on the roof: Balzac, Stendhal, Dickens (when available) and above all Dostoevsky, whose impassioned and obsessive writing seemed to fit the atmosphere of the camp.

There were also various indoor pastimes and activities: lectures, study, card playing, the orchestra, as well as more informal stuff such as seances and political discussions. The latter took up many, many evenings for the others in my room. Frida and Penelope were convinced Communists and Shula was soon converted. Sofka would hold court in her secluded attic room with Shula sitting at her feet, eyes shining as she listened to the gospel of Lenin from the older and more experienced women.

As a Russian princess, Sofka had been considered suitable for marriage to the young Tsarevich, Alexei Nikolaevich, heir to the Russian throne. She had been bundled out of Russia as a child in 1919. Her own conversion to Communism was a thrilling move to make over twenty years later at Vittel. As she herself writes in her autobiography: 'It was these discussions that provided the answer to all those queries and searching that, off and on, had so disturbed me. They explained to me an ideology that I felt could eventually provide mankind with an equitable basis for existence that no other theory ever had.'

For my part, I tried to avoid being dragged into these evening discussions that seemed to gather more significance as the nights drew in and our outside activities were increasingly curtailed. I admired my friends for their intensity and their questing for a brave new world. I was fired with many of their beliefs but each time they dramatically declaimed 'the answer' I pulled back. My own schoolgirl searchings over the rights and wrongs of a particular political theory always brought me back to parliamentary socialism, where it seemed to me that the individual was left to chart his own path in his own way without giving up his right to query a faceless outside discipline.

The first time I went to one of the meetings in Sofka's room was not long after the Germans had invaded the Soviet Union. There was great excitement that Stalin was now in the war on the Allied side. Frida sat at the table, banging it with her fist in her excitement.

'Churchill's government must be pushed to open a Second Front in Europe as soon as possible and the Soviets need British and American supplies now. The Fascist sympathizers in those countries mustn't be allowed to stop them from getting through. The war will be won by the Red Army.'

The others agreed. But I was troubled by one major issue.

'Why did the Soviets sign a pact with the Nazis in the first place?' I asked the room. 'That gave Hitler the green light to go to war with Western Europe. In some ways that's why we're all here.'

I was shouted down by a barrage of voices. My friends had all the standard excuses for Stalin's behaviour between 1939 and 1941 but none held water for me. We would always come back to our disagreements over the Nazi–Soviet pact. I felt terribly let down by the Soviet Union and was depressed by my friends' almost blind faith in Stalin: one day virtually the ally of Hitler, the next his sworn enemy. I couldn't forget that until just a few days before, my Communist friends had been ambivalent about what they called the imperialist war. They had certainly not been fully on the Allied side up to then.

Our arguments would go round and round in circles. I enjoyed the company and the fun of listening to the discussions. I had recently discovered the doubtful joys of knitting and would get wool from an elderly Parisian lady in exchange for chocolate. Much to the intense irritation of the others, I would concentrate earnestly on my latest work-in-progress while attempting to debate with them. My first real knitting achievement was a pair of bedroom slippers, with the soles made from the tapestry seat cover of a chair in our hotel foyer, strengthened with strips of pale blue material cut out from a French Army coat from the First World War. If I didn't have my knitting I would just sit there and daydream. My favourite involved a No.13 bus going down the Finchley Road past my home en route to an enormous restaurant displaying mounds of succulent food!

Many of the organized activities took place in the vast spaces of the Casino, which had a huge hall with a good size stage and numerous function rooms. At any given time it could accommodate study classes, orchestra practice and play rehearsals. Miss Derriman, an indefatigable headmistress figure, arranged a whole series of classes, lectures and study groups, ranging from Russian literature to bookbinding and bee-keeping. I spent a few hellish months tackling German in the rather vague belief that it might come in useful if I managed to escape. By the latter part of the war it was apparently even possible to study for external exams. Madeleine White told me later she had sat her entrance exam for the Sorbonne. She had travelled to Paris, handcuffed and accompanied by German guards, and had stayed for three nights with her aunt before returning to Vittel.

A reasonably competent orchestra was set up by a quiet and refined Frenchwoman. She helped us to produce some less painful but still hair-raising variations on the themes of Mozart and Beethoven. No longer were our concerts given, as at Besançon, in the ramshackle outhouse normally used for peeling potatoes and carrots, with skins slippery on the wet floor and curtains made from mattress covers. They now took place in a proper concert hall where a few loyal music lovers sat and listened to us.

I'm sure that the discipline of practising was a great stimulus. But I fear that in my particular case the results were definitely not worthy of the effort. I could only be described at best as an enthusiastic violinist. In London before the war I had been a member of the Ernest Read Junior Orchestra which met at the Royal Academy. On one occasion Read had tapped his music stand and shouted in exasperation: 'Someone in the second violins is playing the wrong piece!' He didn't know exactly who it was and therefore could not identify me as the culprit, but I still felt like the man in the old H.M. Bateman drawings.

During my months in the camp a number of revue shows were held in the Casino hall. In all this mass of able-bodied and under-employed women there was plenty of professional talent. Apart from the Bluebell girls, there were many other dancers from all over Europe, singers and musicians from the Paris Conservatoire and the Paris Opéra, conjurers, acrobats, actresses, directors and stage designers. The revues were popular with the German officers and guards. A highlight for me was to hear Shula singing Jewish songs while our German captors hummed along appreciatively, blissfully unaware of their origin!

At the weekends we had the cinema to look forward to. I loved the French films with the major stars of the time, such as the comic Fernandel with his horse-like teeth and the sultry Michèle Morgan. At first the German authorities tried to use these films as an opportunity to slip in Nazi propaganda shorts. These showed the smiling faces of people joining hands in one great crusade to inspire the rest of Europe with the glories of Hitler's regime. They were regularly met by a barrage of hoots, whistles and catcalls. They were soon dropped. After this we were subjected to a series of sugary romances between a blond Siegfried and his equally blonde Gretel. These in turn were greeted by our 'Ooohs!' and 'Aaahs!' of exaggerated delight. The first time this happened, a lady sitting in the row in front turned round. She was one of the Kommandant's representatives, Miss Bannister, with whom I had had a number of run-ins.

'Do you mind being quiet,' she said crossly. 'You're interrupting the film. Goodness knows, I would have thought that we could all do with a bit of harmless romance.'

Shula and I giggled, which enraged her even more. We weren't going to stop making fun of the film but in the interest of diplomacy I decided to make sure that we were seated well away from Miss Bannister for the next show.

Seances were one of the strangest activities that flourished from the beginning of our time at Vittel. Many people became deeply and totally committed. Perhaps such involvement answered a real human need to come to terms with being alone and cut off from family. Many people had lost relatives and friends, killed or missing in the war. I don't know if occultism flourished in England at this time but at Vittel it was rife. Even our room was not immune to its appeal. Olga was deeply involved. After what must have been the second or third session she asked me if I would like to join them.

'I'd love to but I'm a bit worried about what will happen.'

'Don't worry, Pat. You don't have to go into a trance. We're doing one tomorrow after dinner.'

So I went along. Quite aside from my natural curiosity, my attitude was one of 'you never know', and it would be nice to believe I could be in touch with my family, even if only the dead ones. The room was lit by just one candle and there were about a dozen women taking part. They all seemed to be elderly apart from us. No one took on the role of medium. This was probably just as well: a disembodied voice and ectoplasm in that greenhouse atmosphere might have rendered some of the more easily impressed women quite hysterical.

I found it all rather predictable but the joggings of the table produced emotional responses from many of those present. Towards the end of the session the cards were read by a woman who looked as though she was about ninety. The message she deciphered barely made sense to me but most seemed to find it all very significant and encouraging. I was disillusioned with the whole affair and never went back, much to Olga's disappointment.

Fortune telling was also extremely popular and it was always very optimistic. Perhaps it had to be so. After all, a palmist in a wartime prison camp could hardly refuse to continue her prophecies just because of what she thought she saw in the hand before her. Olga persuaded me to have my palm read by a sweet old lady from Provence. But there was little substance to it. It was all very general and upbeat. 'Tout va bien, tout va bien,' I remember her repeating.

By the autumn, the focus of interest for many was the show that we were hoping to put on at Christmas in the Casino. Sofka arranged a meeting to form a dramatic society and around fifty of us turned up. Inevitably, we spent a long time arguing about what we should stage.

'What about Aristophanes's *Lysistrata*?' I suggested as we went round in circles thinking of plays. This suggestion produced a mass of blank faces.

'Look,' I went on. 'The cast is entirely female and it's all about a conspiracy of women who refuse to have sex with their husbands until the men stop fighting.'

'It's a classic tale of female survival,' Frida added enthusiastically. 'It's really appropriate for the camp and very funny.'

But we were virtually alone in our choice of play. In fact I don't remember anyone apart from Frida even discussing it. The talk went quickly back to more jolly, predictable Christmas choices and at last we all agreed on *Ali Baba*. Sofka was appointed director of the production, mainly in view of her years spent as Laurence Olivier's secretary and helper before the war. We reasoned she must have picked up some tips along the way. My room-mate Penelope cheerfully agreed to provide all the scenery. As a former teacher of art, she had been allowed to set up a studio in the Casino and had gathered around her many budding sculptors and painters (and some pretty good professionals as well).

I volunteered to work on the small committee that was going to write the show. We had our first meeting a couple of days later and quickly established our intentions. We wanted to insert plenty of English and French songs and ditties with double meanings and a few of Shula's Jewish songs. We wondered how much would be allowed.

'Do you think the censor will pass "It's a Long Way to Tipperary"?'

'We could try,' I said. 'What about "Roll Out the Barrel"? Perhaps he'll miss the bit about having the Huns on the run.'

There were hoots of laughter at this. The meeting was fun and we had a good outline of the show by the end of it. Nevertheless, I went to only one more. My heart was never really in it: by this time I was planning to escape and I fervently hoped that I wouldn't be around for the actual performance. I let the others fight over the details of who would star in what scene, which costumes could be produced and how they would light and stage the whole production.

It was as we were leaving that first meeting that I overheard someone making a disparaging comment in French. It was directed at Frida and me. It was to the effect that 'those English' always think they know best but they don't. This wasn't the first time that I had heard dark mutterings that the 'proper' Englishwomen were receiving preferential treatment from the Germans. I had heard similar remarks after our first journey to Besançon, when it had been claimed that we had been given the best seats on the train. Perhaps my friendly reception from the Kommandant and his officers at work was a reflection of this? They had all seemed suitably impressed that my father was a retired Lieutenant-Commander of the Royal Navy.

I gained a new perspective on this matter from a letter I received years later from Madeleine White, who talked about a side of the camp that I had never experienced. Madeleine's mother married an English Tommy after the First World War and they separated some months after her birth. There was very little money on her mother's side. Madeleine visited her father's relatives in England quite frequently but was essentially French in her outlook. She was interned with her mother, who felt she could never ask for anything and consequently did not get any of the better shoes or clothes as they became available. Madeleine found that the larger rooms went to the 'real English,' she wrote, not to the ones 'like us, who know little of English life and customs, and have not been brought up in English schools'.

If we were treated more favourably by our captors I was certainly unaware of it at the time. I could not have believed that persistent troublemakers such as Frida and myself could have been given preferential treatment. Just the opposite! After all, I was never allowed a trip into town at either of the camps to see the dentist or doctor. Indeed, we were convinced that we had been put in the quarters on the top floor of the hotel precisely to lessen the possibility of our making the kind of trouble at which we had become expert at Besançon.

If the passing months engendered quarrels and jealousies amongst us, they also produced for many a growing lack of concentration or an inability to see a project or discussion through to the end. This is probably the bugbear of every prisoner. I found that the hours began to lag for me, regardless of the various activities that were on offer.

It would also depress me to see the nutters in their obsessive and pathetic wanderings around the park. One woman would continually recite Shakespeare. Another reverted to childhood, speaking in a baby's voice. Battered by life in late middle age, they found our prison a comfort rather than a challenge. Such people would be easily recognized, I imagine, in any sort of prison. They were apprehensive of release, with its demands on the individual and the withdrawal of comforting rules and regulations. As they trailed their paper bags, talking and singing to themselves, letting go by the board the basic ideas of cleanliness and personal care, they were neither unhappy nor scared. I hated to see the German soldiers laughing at them.

It was vital not to sink into the lifestyle of such women. 'What does it matter?' they would cry. 'Just look after yourself and get what you can.' The motto of the camp for many seemed to be 'It could be much worse.' Indeed it could. Remembering back to the days of Besançon, this place was better fitted out than many ordinary homes. With a bathroom across our corridor shared with just one other room, we were a long way from our former conditions with a single cold-water tap serving perhaps twenty inmates in a bug-ridden dormitory with open toilets in the courtyard.

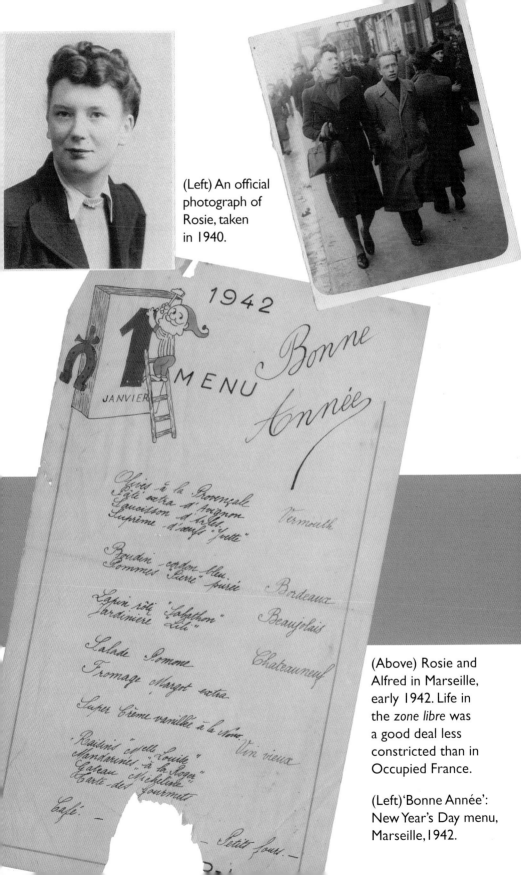

(Left) An official photograph of Rosie, taken in 1940.

(Above) Rosie and Alfred in Marseille, early 1942. Life in the *zone libre* was a good deal less constricted than in Occupied France.

(Left) 'Bonne Année': New Year's Day menu, Marseille, 1942.

Striking, generous, irrepressible: Nancy Wake. The Australian SOE agent, a key figure in the French Resistance, befriended Rosie in Marseille.

Rosemary is 'very well': letter from Hoytie Wiborg to Commander Say, January 1942.

HOTEL BRISTOL

Rua de S. Pedro de Alcântara, 81

JARDIM
LISBOA

TELEFONE P. B. X.
2 2084

ALBERTO ARAÚJO
Proprietário

Jan. 18ᵗʰ 1942

R. Say Eyr. 42 Pallison Rd. London

Dear Mr Say —, I left your daughter Rosemary in Marseilles barely a week ago, crossing Spain and Portugal via Cerbère, Port Bou and Valencia d'Alcantara, as she will come, as soon as her Portuguese and Spanish "Visas" arrive — I promised I would write to you, as she does not wish for to worry about her. She and Dick Stewart, her travelling companion, are both very well cheerful and taking light of all their adventures! I have been so in admiration of their courage and spirit after the many months of terrific hardships they suffered — But it is in no wise affected their health or spirits — and you must be assured of this so as not to worry — As to their visas I look for the number of the telegram sent to

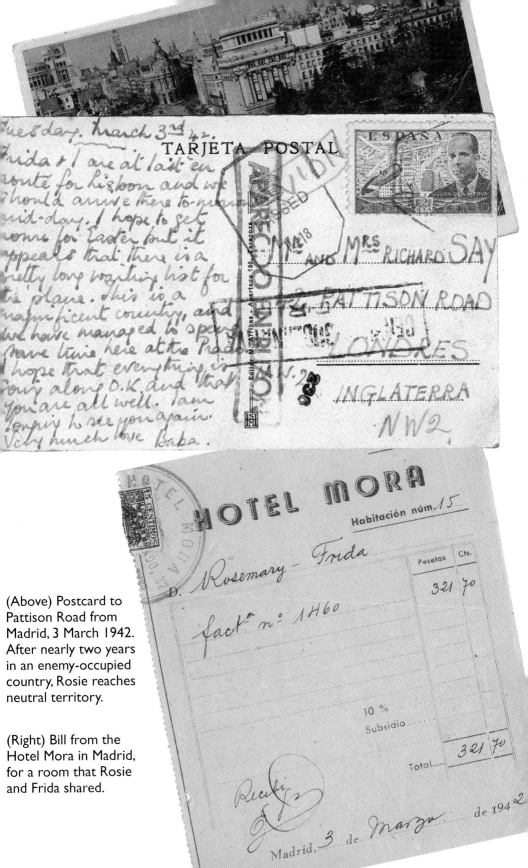

Tuesday. March 3rd 42.

Frida & I are at last en route for Lisbon and we should arrive there to-morrow mid-day. I hope to get home for Easter but it appears that there is a pretty long waiting list for the plane. This is a magnificent country, and we have managed to spend some time here at the Prado. I hope that everything is going along O.K. and that you are all well. I am longing to see you again. Very much love Baba.

TARJETA POSTAL

... AND Mrs RICHARD SAY
... PATTISON ROAD
... LONDRES
INGLATERRA
NW2

HOTEL MORA

Habitación núm. 15

D. Rosemary — Frida

factª nº 1460

	Pesetas	Cts.
	321	70
10 % Subsidio		
Total	321	70

Madrid, 3 de Marzo de 1942

(Above) Postcard to Pattison Road from Madrid, 3 March 1942. After nearly two years in an enemy-occupied country, Rosie reaches neutral territory.

(Right) Bill from the Hotel Mora in Madrid, for a room that Rosie and Frida shared.

BRITISH OVERSEAS AIRWAYS CORPORATION

TELEGRAMS: FLYING, LONDON   Reference: LO.TP.5439   AIRWAYS HOUSE,
TELEPHONE: VICTORIA 2323.   LONDON, S.W. 1.

31st January, 1942.

Commander Richard Say, R.N.V.R.,
Room 114B,
West Block III,
Admiralty, S.W.1.

Dear Sir,

<u>Miss Rosemary Say and</u>
<u>Miss Frida Stewart.</u>

We thank you for your letter of the 30th January, from which we note that you may wish us to arrange the journey of the above ladies from Lisbon to this country.

Owing to Government requirements, there is a waiting list for the Lisbon/United Kingdom service, and although the position has eased somewhat, prospective passengers may anticipate some little delay in Lisbon waiting for a connection to this country.

The single fare for this journey amounts to £35 15s. 6d.,

/and....

- 2 -

and upon receipt of the appropriate remittance we shall be pleased to write to our Lisbon Office, instructing them to register the names of these ladies on the waiting list and to issue the tickets on application.

It is noted that your daughter and her friend are at present in the care of the American Consul at Marseilles, and in the circumstances we suggest you let us telegraph to the Consul confirming the payment of fares for the journey Lisbon/United Kingdom, as this will undoubtedly facilitate the granting of visas etc. The extra charge would amount to 10s., and perhaps you will kindly include this sum with your remittance if you wish us to do this.

With regard to the final paragraph of your letter, the present state of the waiting list does not warrant priority being obtained, but should you wish to make application for preferential treatment for these ladies we suggest you approach the Air Ministry through the C.W. Branch of the Admiralty.

We now look forward to receiving your further instructions in this connection.

Yours faithfully,

J.B. Franklin

for Senior Traffic Officer.

£35. 15s. 6d.: the single-fare journey from Lisbon to the UK.

Twenty-eight balls of wool:
a receipt from John Smith's
drapery in Adare, Co. Limerick.

Rosie's telegram to her father on arriving at Bournemouth,
following the flight from Ireland to Poole, March 1942.

They Arrived in London To-day From France

Miss Freda Stewart (left) and her companion, Miss Rosemary Say, on arrival in London to-day.—Evening Standard picture.

TWO WOMEN ESCAPED FROM NAZI CAMP

Evening Standard Reporter

Two women who escaped from a Nazi internment camp at Vittel in Occupied France stepped out of the train in London to-day as cheerfully as if they were just back from a Continental holiday.

They were 31-year-old Freda Stewart and Rosemary (Pat) Say, 23. They were fit and laughing.

Rosemary flung her arms round her father, Commander Say, R.N., and Freda hugged her sister, who had come to London to meet her from their home in Cambridge.

Good Things to Eat

There were greetings too, for Mrs. Say and for sister Joan Say, in her A.T.S. officer's uniform.

The girls, hatless, arrived with big suitcases and string bags filled with pineapples and other good things from Lisbon. Miss Stewart ,dark-haired and

(Continued on Back Page, Col. Two)

They Escaped From France

(Continued from PAGE ONE)

blue-eyed, who was working in a refugee organisation in Paris when the Nazis marched in, said:

"We may be looking gay and fit enough now—but that's the food at Lisbon. When we were rounded up by the Nazis in December 1940 we were sent to the famous camp at Besançon, where the conditions were unspeakable.

"There were no sanitary arrangements, and very little food.

A Spot of Grease

"At Vittel conditions were a little better, but food was very scarce—just a meagre vegetable soup for lunch, and in the evening a spot of grease with our bread, or a piece of ersatz cheese or a little ersatz jam.

"Pat and I agreed that we didn't like it so we made plans to escape. We packed a few necessary belongings in small suitcases.

"We got away by crawling through a hole in a barbed wire fence.

"That dark morning when we wriggled through the wire we took a big chance when we walked past the sentry.

"He flashed a torch on us, but evidently thought we were peasant women and he did not stop us. After that it was easy."

Train to Marseilles

I asked if they had any difficulty about their passports and identification papers when going through the villages of Occupied France.

"That was—arranged," said Miss Say, who told me that they took the train for Marseilles just like ordinary passengers.

'As if they were just back from a Continental holiday': report on the front page of the London *Evening Standard*, 14 March 1942. Rosie clutches a string bag containing a pineapple purchased in Lisbon.

any further communication
on this subject, please quote

No. K 4237/3/248.

and address—

not to any person by name
but to—

"The Under-Secretary of State,"
Foreign Office,
London, S.W.I.

FOREIGN OFFICE.

S.W.1.

29th May, 1943.

Madam,

With reference to your letter of the 4th May regarding the amount of your indebtedness to His Majesty's Government for advances made to you in connexion with your repatriation expenses, I am directed by His Majesty's Principal Secretary of State for Foreign Affairs to inform you that, as far as is at present known, the total amount due from you is £64. 1s. 9d., made up as follows:—

Marseilles	£39.	0s.	0d.
Barcelona	8.	16s.	2d.
Madrid	5.	18s.	3d.
Lisbon	10.	7s.	4d.
	£64.	1s.	9d.

2. This total does not include any advances which you may have received in occupied France, particulars of which are not yet available.

I am,
Madam,
Your obedient Servant,

Miss R. Say,
5, Albany Terrace,
Regents Park,
N.W.1.

Madam,

With reference to the letters from this department of 29th May and 26th July, to which no answers have been received, I am directed by His Majesty's Principal Secretary of State for Foreign Affairs to inform you that if you do not immediately reply to this and any future letters, it will be necessary for this department to consider without further notice what other measures may have to be adopted in order to secure repayment of the expenses of your repatriation.

I am,
Madam,
Your obedient Servant,

(Above) Indebted to HMG: letter from the Foreign Office regarding repatriation expenses.

(Left) The battle over Rosie's debt: the Foreign Office warns of 'other measures'.

Rosie and Robert (Bobby) Hawkings at Pattison Road, 1942.

Rosie and Ricardo, September 1944.

This is the life: Rosie and Ricardo in Madrid.

But how and when would we ever get out? The news in October that Moscow was apparently on the brink of falling to the Germans was particularly depressing for me. I had never believed that Churchill would make peace with Hitler, even in the likely event that the Red Army was defeated. If that were the case, the war might simply grind to a stalemate. The appalling thought occurred to me that we could be stuck in this stifling atmosphere for perhaps years. I began to think more and more of escaping.

CHAPTER TWELVE

Thoughts of Leaving

'What about disguising ourselves as French workmen?'

'You're mad, Shula,' I said. 'What about your bust? In case you haven't noticed, French workmen don't have one.'

'Well, I think we'd still have a good chance of reaching the border without getting caught. If we could only get out.'

'How are we going to get there? Switzerland's about fifty miles away.'

'Oh, I don't know, Patachoun. There must be trains running to it. Once we're there we could get across. I don't suppose tracking down escaped English girls is going to be the highest priority for the German Army.'

I was curled up on my bunk one afternoon arguing with Shula about escaping. Her logic seemed to be impeccable. While we knew we were fortunate to have a Kommandant who was too old for service on the Russian Front and who wanted no trouble, it was a different thing to slip away from under his nose. There would be nothing dramatic like being shot at dawn if we were caught. But as sure as sure, we would be working in a German munitions factory with other forced labour prisoners. He had to maintain his authority. You can't be made a fool of.

We seemed to speculate endlessly as the weeks went by. Sometimes it was Shula who was optimistic, sometimes me. The Kommandant and his officers were always reminding us how difficult it was to escape from any German POW camp. And we always got stuck on the question of where we should make for once we were outside. It was particularly galling that practically all the other Commonwealth citizens had been released by the summer. As I wrote to my sister Joan: '. . . why weren't we born in Ottawa, Honey? Or even Sydney would have got me out long ago . . . '

My vague plans were made real one lovely autumn day as I was walking around the grounds with Frida. We had often talked about the possibilities of escape but, as with Shula, our discussions had never got very far. Until now, when she made a surprising revelation.

'If we could somehow get out of the camp,' she told me, 'I have contacts who may be able to get us across the Swiss border. But it would mean going back to Besançon, of all places. Are you interested in coming with me, Pat?'

'Of course I am. I'd do practically anything to get out. But why Besançon?'

'Do you remember hearing about the dentist there who'd congratulate British patients on the latest RAF raids as he filled their teeth?'

'Yes, but no one knew if he was serious or not.'

'Well, he is. I've had it confirmed that he's willing to help escapees.'

I gulped. I was slightly taken aback by the suddenness of it all. But I had made my decision a long time ago: I was desperate to get out. So, by the time the curfew whistle was sounded we had already worked out the beginnings of a plan.

We agreed on a number of things. First, we needed money. We would write home, asking our parents to send money orders, and we'd start selling our possessions and Red Cross supplies – especially the cigarettes. Second, we would inform no one else of our plans unless absolutely necessary. Words slipped out inadvertently and they could easily be picked up by the professional gossips and slanderers who roamed the camp. Third, we would need to get hold of our passports (to get into Switzerland) and false documents for travel within France (the dentist in Besançon could, we hoped, provide papers). Finally, we would keep an open mind on the actual method of escape. Perhaps some of the French workmen who came daily into the camp would be able to help us here. The important thing was to be ready to go. At once, if necessary.

Over the next few days, therefore, we began to look in earnest for different ways of escaping. The tenor of our lives now changed: we were no longer inventing mad schemes that would end in giggles and laughter or going round in circles and ending up frustrated. We scoured the wire fencing to find the most suitable place to climb through without wire cutters.

We discussed approaching one of the workmen. This proved to be much more difficult than we had at first thought. There was a worrying amount of double-dealing and spying going on in Vittel. No one was confident that those men who proclaimed anti-German feelings were really sincere. In fact, the Kommandant boasted that he had a whole network of spies both inside and outside the camp. We couldn't be sure if he was telling the truth. I had made friends with the small team of French prisoners who worked in the office with me but most of them were family men who made it very clear that they did not want to do more than their allotted shift.

From what she had told me about the dentist in Besançon, I guessed that Frida had Communist contacts outside the camp who could help us. I never asked her about them and Frida didn't volunteer information. Curiously, this was something that was never at any point to be discussed in our many decades of friendship after the war.

I have often wondered why Frida asked me to go with her and not one of her close political friends such as Penelope, Olga or Sofka. They would certainly have been more in tune with her. While I liked Frida a lot we were very different. She was nearly ten years older than me and a far more reflective, thinking person. I knew she considered me something of an undependable flibbertigibbet. Nevertheless, we turned out to be a good team over the coming months. I never did find out why she chose me.

The search for an escape route lasted a couple of weeks but without success. Our enthusiasm and energy rapidly dried up as we came into November. The weather turned cold and we began to get disheartened. Perhaps we had left it too late? The air was freezing and the first snows not far away. To make matters worse, my old trouble with bronchitis had started up again. Whoever heard of a prisoner escaping with a hacking cough?

One day a band of workmen arrived to put the various hotels' central heating in order for the coming winter. On our floor we had a cheerful, elderly man called Alain. He spoke good sailor's English. He had served in the merchant fleet for years and spent the first day gaily recounting stories of the dockland bars and brothels in places such as Tilbury, Southampton, and Liverpool. That night Frida and I decided that we would confide in him.

'I'd like to get back to London before the war ends,' I said to him the next morning as he was mending the radiator in our room.

He had just finished telling me a long story about a visit he had made there in the early 1920s. I mentioned my wish in a very offhand way. I didn't want to commit myself. His eyes gleamed.

'If Mademoiselle really wants to go,' he said, 'I can help you. There is a sewer pipe at the back of this hotel. It will lead you outside the camp. I know it well. I have worked on the sewers here.'

My heart sank at the prospect of struggling though miles of filthy tunnels which were probably full of rats. Still, it was an idea. 'And then what?' I asked.

'Very simple. It is three or four days' march to Belfort. Then you are near the Swiss border. I have a brother there who will help you.'

I wasn't very enthusiastic. Nevertheless, I discussed it later with Frida on our regular pre-curfew walk around the grounds.

'Great,' she said, after I had told her Alain's plan. 'We crawl through the filthy sewers and then trudge for three days in our stinking, wet clothes across the countryside into the foothills of the Juras. We're escapees, Pat, not martyrs.'

We both burst out laughing at the absurdity of the idea. We'd have to think of something else. The next afternoon our money orders from home came through at last. Mine arrived with a typical note from my father advising me not to be extravagant in the camp but to save my money for later. Little did he know how economical I had been. I had been reduced to chewing the sour regulation loaves, as everything we could sell had been advertised on the exchange and mart board. Even my beautiful ski suit and boots had gone. We had about 1,000 francs between us (almost £250 today). We thought that this would be enough to last a week or so. I approached our friend again the following day.

'We need to go soon, Alain, or the weather will be totally against us. But we're not keen on the sewers idea. Is there no other way of getting out?'

He grinned slyly. 'My friend is working this week in the Casino. Maybe he gives you some keys. You hide there at night, cut the wires and go on the early train. He tells me there is no control on it.'

I rushed to tell Frida. This seemed promising, at the very least. Why hadn't we thought of the Casino before? For some reason we had always ignored that building on our previous scouting missions. As soon as we could we walked over there and began to search around. The Casino was part of the spa complex and looked on to the park and our hotel. The rear of the building abutted the barbed-wire perimeter fence and a main road beyond it. We discovered that the small outhouse at the rear was now being used as a coalbunker. From a distance it looked as if the barbed wire had been disturbed, probably to allow the coal lorry to get through.

Was this really the weak point in the camp security where we could try to get out? If it was, it would mean spending the night in the outhouse and cutting the barbed wire at the moment of changeover for the sentries. Once we got through the perimeter fence we would be on the road to the station and the town. The main gate to the camp and the guardroom would be on our left. So we wouldn't have to go through them from the camp itself but we would still have to pass right by. With any luck we would be taken for French workers. We would need two keys from our helper: one for the front door of the Casino and one for the door leading to the outhouse.

We were both incredibly excited by this discovery. We would go for it. We walked around the grounds talking and planning. We knew there was no problem being out after curfew, as we had often slipped out in the evening. We needed someone to cover our tracks after we had escaped. She would have to stay the night in the coal bunker with us. We decided to ask Penelope. We explained to her that once we were through, we needed her to take the wire cutter, fasten the window and make her way back to the Casino, locking the door of the outhouse behind her. She would have to wait until the night curfew was lifted, unlock the door of the Casino and slip back to her bedroom at the Grand Hotel in time for the morning roll call. Alain would pick up the keys and the wire cutter from her. She readily agreed.

That was it. We were going the following night. We sat down to plan our route. We knew from the workmen that there was an early morning train for Épinal, just a few miles away. From the map it looked as if we would have to go further north from there on a branch line to the large town of Nancy. And from Nancy there was a direct train south to Besançon. Our route seemed to involve a lot of travelling and changing of trains. We would have to place our trust in Alain's assurance that there really were no German controls on the train, even in this part of Occupied France so close to the German border.

How could we make sure that our three room-mates weren't blamed for our escape? They needed an alibi of sorts for the evening. Penelope, who was organizing the sets and costumes for the Christmas pantomime, suggested that Shula and Olga work in the main foyer helping Sofka to design costumes. She calculated that anyone around would also assume that she was working with them, given that she had made such a fuss about being in charge of the whole thing.

We were right to be concerned about our friends, as the Kommandant did indeed take retribution on them. But, as we learnt some years later, the girls succeeded in turning his punishment into a farce. Once our absence was noticed, they were called to the Kommandant's office. They claimed ignorance of our movements. Regardless of this, they were escorted by two sentries to a small guard house and locked up with a sentry on duty outside. They were to stay there until they were ready to inform the Kommandant of our whereabouts. There was one outside lavatory, which they used in a constant procession throughout the night, banging on the door to waken the sentry every few minutes. He had to unlock the door and accompany them one after the other to the outhouse. In the morning they hung out of the windows shouting for food. By sheer chance there was a Red Cross delegation due that afternoon and the Kommandant could not afford this unwelcome diversion. They were all let out.

The last thing we needed to work out was how to make sure that our escape went undetected by the authorities for as long as possible. After all, I worked every morning at the Kommandant's office – my absence there would be queried immediately. We decided that the best thing was for me to take to my bed. The following day after I finished work, Frida would pass the word to the office that I had gone down with food poisoning. That should give me a couple of days' grace. We also had to have someone to cover for both of us at the morning roll call, which was a bit of a mumbling occasion. I found Shula drawing by the steps of our hotel. She wasn't particularly surprised at my news.

'I'll miss you terribly, Patachoun,' she said, holding my hand. 'But you'll succeed. Forget you're English once you're out of here. Talk and think in French. You speak it like a native anyway.' Paradoxically, her optimism made me feel defensive and defeatist.

'But we don't even look French. What about my height? And teeth? I look more German, if anything.'

'You'll be fine. Switzerland's not far.'

'Oh, I don't know if we're doing the right thing, Shula. What about my parents? Should I put them through any more? It might be months before they get any word from us. They'll be worried stiff.'

I was, in truth, beginning to panic about the escape. Whether we would succeed was all a question of chance: either we would be lucky or we would be dispatched to work in a German munitions factory. After all, we had no false papers and not much money. We weren't even sure if we could travel on the trains. And my cough! It came in waves – a hard, barking sound. It made me feel very conspicuous.

I went to bed that night dreaming I was a child again, walking over the Norfolk fields and shouting at my family to wait for me. My jacket had caught on a barbed wire fence and I couldn't move. I woke up in the dark of early morning and lay in bed worrying. I knew that there was no backing down. We had made our decision. We were going that night.

CHAPTER THIRTEEN

Escape

I had long planned how to get our passports from the Kommandant's office. I knew I was trusted with routine paperwork and felt I could easily pick them up without anybody querying why I was there and what I was doing. That morning, almost fainting with tension and fear, I walked over to the cupboard in the anteroom and quietly removed our passports. There were hundreds of other documents there. Ours would never be missed until we were well away from the camp.

'Fräulein Say. Can you file these papers please?'

I turned round. A soldier was staring at me and holding a raft of documents. I must have looked like a dead fish gaping at the man.

'Are you all right, Fräulein?'

With a huge effort I closed my mouth and smiled. 'Of course,' I said, taking the papers and putting them with the passports. I walked out of the room. I couldn't help feeling that as an escapee I had some way to go in the confidence stakes.

Later that afternoon Alain confirmed to us that as far as he knew the Germans had not, as yet, put any checks on passengers for the Épinal train. 'You'll have to settle in the outhouse before curfew,' he said as he handed us the keys. 'There'll be a few minutes for you to get away when the sentries do their changeover.'

I couldn't help one last moan. 'Alain, we're going to freeze lying in there.'

'Well, with a bit of luck the sentries will think the same way and toddle off to the guardroom for a hot drink and some warmth,' Frida countered quickly. She grabbed her coat and a piece of paper and strode towards the door.

'Anyway, I'd better go and see our friend Servais,' she said. 'He'd be really suspicious if I didn't turn up for our daily musical battle. Nothing must seem out of the ordinary on the day we escape. Let's leave with one more small triumph against Nazi propaganda. See you later.'

With a smile she was gone. Frida had taken it upon herself to provide a daily list of suggested music to be played over the tannoy of the camp. Although Jewish composers such as Mendelssohn were still banned, she tried to get as many Polish or Russian pieces played as possible. Her latest success was Borodin. That Germany was now at war with the Soviet Union had apparently not been noticed by Servais.

When she got back we made final preparations alone in our room. We parcelled out our remaining possessions for the others, left them a note saying that we were just about in our right minds and set off downstairs. At the entrance to the hotel we met one of the British women who helped to run the camp. She looked at us with obvious disdain.

'You realize that it's nearly seven, I presume? The curfew whistle will be going in a few minutes. Make sure you're back on time.'

'We're just going to get some air, Miss Short,' I said. 'We'll be back.' We slipped into the Casino where Penelope was already waiting for us.

'Quick, you two,' she whispered. 'The chorus girls are still rehearsing in the hall. Let's hide here.'

We stayed in the shadows. We had forgotten about the chorus girls. In a matter of minutes they put out the lights and left. We heard the curfew whistle. In pitch dark we tiptoed to the outhouse. Penelope unlocked the communicating door and went inside. We heard her trip and swear quietly.

'Wait a sec,' she said. We could vaguely make out her figure as she felt her way around. We heard something shift. 'Watch out. There's coal everywhere.'

We hadn't asked ourselves beforehand what a coal bunker was really like to spend the night in. Now we knew: there were mountains and valleys of the stuff. Frida went in and set off what seemed like an avalanche.

'Damn, this stuff here's coke not coal. It slides about if it's even touched.'

The three of us found an empty bit of floor and sat down gingerly. We daren't lean against the coal, for fear of setting it off. The floor was too dirty to lie on. So we had to sit bolt upright.

'We've got ages ahead of us,' Penelope whispered. 'I don't know if I can stay like this. The freezing cold will give us cramp.'

But there was no point in complaining – we were going to be here for about ten hours. Had the sentries heard the noise from the coal? We had to stay still and quiet all night. Somehow this didn't seem the most heroic of escapes. I began to doze, fitfully waking up as I toppled over in my sleep.

'Pat!' Frida hissed. She pinched her nose. 'You're snoring.'

I looked at my watch. It was just gone eleven. I didn't sleep or even doze again that night. I started to get awful cramp in my calves and did some foot-curling exercises to try to get some circulation going. My toes were numb. I started to worry about my cough. Shula had given me a packet of lozenges from the nuns' pharmacy and I got through the whole lot. I survived the wait without a serious bout of coughing. In retrospect, I think that my worries about cramp and bronchitis helped me to get through the night. They certainly diverted my mind away from fear or boredom.

As dawn approached I was wide awake with my mind racing. This really was the beginning of my journey home. I could see my parents' front door. I imagined myself walking up the road to Hampstead Heath. Just then I heard the sentries not far off. They were laughing and slapping their arms against their bodies to keep warm. Frida listened intently to hear what they were saying. Their voices faded away. She nodded.

This was our opportunity. We had been banking on the fact that they would go to the guardroom to have a drink and get warm. The handover to their replacements would probably take a few minutes. Frida moved cautiously. She stifled a yell of cramp pain and eased up to the window above her head. She groaned.

'Damn! It's all off,' she whispered. 'It's been snowing. They'll see our tracks leading from the hut.'

I couldn't believe it. It was just our luck that the first snow of the year had fallen on our escape day. I was so exhausted after a night of sitting upright that I could hardly think. But I knew that this was our one chance. We had to go now.

I clambered up to the window and peered into the murky light. In fact there wasn't much snow on the cinder track that led from the outhouse to the fence. So perhaps our footprints might not be seen after all.

I gently opened the window and climbed out. I ran the few yards to the fence. To my disbelief I found that the wire had been cut to allow the lorry through and then merely looped back in place. Presumably the driver had to make regular deliveries. He had probably thought that with the guardroom so near there was no risk of any prisoner escaping by this route. I was shaking with excitement as I returned to the window and told them what I had seen.

'There's hardly any snow on the path, so we can get to the fence without being noticed. There'll be people walking on the road on the other side. Nobody will see our footprints. Let's go.'

We said our goodbyes to Penelope. She squeezed my hand but said nothing. Frida scrambled out of the window and darted over to the fence. She turned to me and I ran to join her. I lifted up the cut fence to let her through. As I did, the edge of the wire I was holding got caught with the wire above. It looked as if it would hold to let me through. Frida waited on the other side of the wire, looking around anxiously. Just as I stepped through, the top wire released its hold and I felt the sharp jaws bite into my coat.

I was caught. Somehow I had known that this would happen. I froze. But Frida didn't panic for one moment. She eased the prong out of my coat with her long, bony fingers. We heard the sounds of footsteps not far away. She pulled hastily, leaving a piece of coat on the wire. We crouched down. It was about six o'clock and the sky was lightening a little. In the distance a few early workers were stumbling along the snowy road in the direction of the town and the railway station. Frida carefully pulled the piece of my coat from the wire and looped the fence back. We jumped on to the road where the men had been walking. We looked back at the outhouse: a hand waved and the window closed.

So far so good, except for my damaged coat which might look a bit strange. We tightened our headscarves, picked up our few belongings and began to walk down the road. We could see the big gates of the main entrance on our left. We would have to walk straight past them. We kept our heads down. A bicycle silently passed us. It was a German soldier. I had a horrible vision of us stupidly being caught on our own doorstep and taken back to the camp. He turned down a side road.

We walked on without speaking. It seemed to me that we weren't even moving. I heard someone call across the road to a friend. We were approaching the lighted guardroom at the main gates of the camp. The windows were steamed up. The soldiers inside were eating and drinking with much guffawing. One of them rubbed a clear spot on the window with his hand and peered out. I doubled up in a paroxysm of coughing. It was sheer nerves. Frida put her arm around my shoulder. We walked right by the front gates of our prison.

We reached the station after about ten minutes. We had agreed that I would do the talking wherever possible. Although Frida's French was very good, it was I who could pass for a native. She was going to be our German speaker if (please God it didn't happen) we needed to talk ourselves out of trouble. I bought two tickets for Besançon. The man in the office yawned and handed them to me with my change.

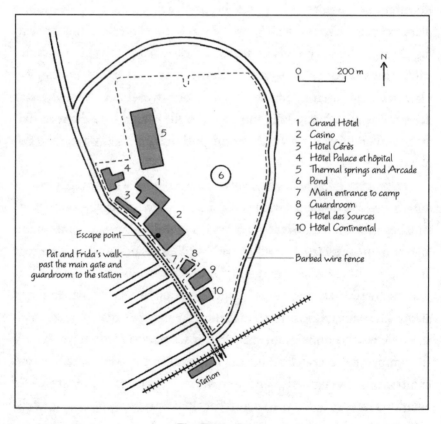

The Escape Route

'You'll need to get the connecting trains at Épinal and Nancy,' he muttered without even looking up.

We walked on to the platform. To my horror the first person I saw was the German head doctor from the camp, standing a few yards away on my left. 'Good God, Frida,' I breathed. 'I went to see him just last week. He's the awful man who's been treating me for bronchitis. You know, the one who told me that the Germans will be in Piccadilly before I leave this camp. Why did I try to persuade him that I should be sent home? He's bound to remember me.'

'No eye contact, that's the secret,' she whispered.

Worse was to follow. I nudged Frida in the ribs. The Kommandant's secretary was deep in conversation further down the platform. She knew us well. We turned our backs to the tracks and gazed fixedly at the worn posters on the platform wall. Time seemed to stand still. Where was the train? We could hear people walking along the platform behind us. Was one of them the doctor? Or the secretary? The urge to turn round was almost irresistible. I stared as hard as I could at the poster advertising Vittel water. If I didn't look at anyone, perhaps nobody would see me – the ostrich method of escape!

When the train finally arrived we moved quickly down to the other end of the platform. It was getting lighter all the time. We got into a small, closed compartment. The train slowly moved away from Vittel. We looked at each other, hardly breathing. We had done it. Until Épinal, at least.

We slunk off the train about an hour later, looking apprehensively at the disembarking passengers. There were none that we knew. We showed our tickets and walked into the town without speaking. We had the whole day to wait before our connection for Nancy. We felt an exhilarating freedom: for the first time in almost a year we were able simply to wander around a town, drinking in the life. The sounds and the smells were so strange. And the queues! Outside all the food shops were long lines of weary housewives, dressed in shabby clothes and holding huge baskets. It was only after perhaps an hour that we began to worry that the place was full of Germans in uniform, presumably on leave.

Two soldiers approached us. I clung to Frida's arm, trying to hide my torn coat. The taller of the two took out a packet of cigarettes and offered one to me. He smiled broadly and said: 'Promenade, Mademoiselle?'

I shook my head and held on to Frida even more tightly. We moved away.

'Let's get out of here,' Frida said. 'We're too obvious. No one else is just walking these streets.'

She was right. There were no other civilians sauntering along looking at shops. We needed to get inside somewhere, away from people if possible. It was bitterly cold and had started to snow. By now we were feeling exhausted from the lack of sleep and the high nervous energy of the escape. We slipped into a small church down a side street and sat on the hard pews at the back. At that time of the morning it was totally deserted. Trying to look devout, we bent our heads and began to divide up our meagre portions of hard biscuits and cold potatoes. Within a few minutes the pews began to fill up for morning mass.

'Don't worry,' I whispered to Frida. 'I know all the forms of service from my sessions with the nuns.'

She didn't look totally convinced. As a bell tinkled I nudged her to stand. She shot up, wiping the last crumbs from her coat. The rest of the congregation promptly knelt down. This was clearly no place for us. I started to cough violently. By sheer luck, I couldn't have done anything better: I became just another person trying to cope with a consumptive cough in that cold church. We made our way out as unobtrusively as possible.

We were still faced with the problem of how to pass the hours before our connection to Nancy. We had to get off the streets. After a while we succumbed to a warm cafe in a bleak, lonely part of town. We made our cups of ersatz coffee last as long as we could, sitting opposite each other in an uneasy silence.

By five o'clock we were back at the station and soon installed in a cold and dark carriage which we had to ourselves. We were by now both very sleepy. Just as the train's whistle was blowing, the door was flung open and three boisterous German soldiers piled in. Frida and I looked at each other, horror-struck. We quickly put our heads down and pretended to doze. All thoughts of a real sleep had vanished. They kept up a continual chatter. I could just see that one of them was staring at us and whispering to his friends. I felt my body going rigid and told myself to relax. After all, I was supposed to be asleep. I was desperate to move, to scratch. To our great relief they eventually went out into the corridor where they stood smoking.

'They're saying,' Frida told me, 'that we might go out with them tonight. Just ignore them. I don't think they're that interested.'

She was right. They came back into the compartment and made a few remarks to us in German but we made it clear that we couldn't understand them. The journey was agonizingly long, with the train stopping and starting with depressing regularity. We wouldn't make the connection for Besançon that was for sure.

'We're going to need somewhere to stay in Nancy,' I whispered to Frida in French. 'We can't wait at the station all night.'

'I know, but it's too risky to go to a hotel without papers.'

We sat there, glumly thinking. 'There's nothing for it,' I said at last. 'I'm going to find the guard. Perhaps he can help us.'

We were in luck. The guard was immediately understanding. He told me there was a small hotel near the station that was what he called 'sympatique et respectable'. It could have been a brothel for all I cared. We had started on a journey that already seemed far too long. I huddled into the corner of the carriage and this time I really did doze off, to be wakened by Frida shaking me.

'Nancy. *On arrive.*'

Still only half awake, I climbed down the high carriage steps, anxious to get away from the soldiers. I missed the last step and fell heavily.

'Damn! My ankle . . . I think I've bust it,' I shouted out in clear English.

Frida stared at me horrified. The soldiers were looking out of the carriage windows watching us. We froze for a long moment. After a few seconds they closed the carriage door. They waved as the train pulled away. Very slowly we started to breathe again.

We found the hotel easily. The proprietress was a severe-looking woman who received us without a word. She handed us the registration forms to sign but didn't ask for our papers. We followed her upstairs to our room. Still not speaking, she motioned to two pairs of German army boots placed outside the next bedroom and then left us. We sat on the bed and looked at each other. Well, we had made it, but it didn't look like there was going to be much sleep for us that night. Our unwanted neighbours were hardly conducive to a good rest. And there was always the prospect of a random check on the hotel by the authorities.

'What do you think?' Frida asked. 'Does she suspect we're on the run? She must know the risk she's taking.'

'I don't know. I don't care. I just want to get on the first train to Besançon.'

We had a very fitful night. We woke early the next morning and crept downstairs in the semi-darkness. The place was silent. In the small dining room the proprietress gave us some bread and hot herbal tea.

Yes, she knew all right. It was our first encounter with the stolid resistance of the French towards an occupying army.

'Bonne chance,' she whispered to us as we left, still with absolutely no change of expression.

PART FOUR

The Long Road Home

NOVEMBER 1941 – MARCH 1942

---

[5] The food situation was worsening. Substitute products – known as national or ersatz – were increasingly used. There was bitter resentment at German requisitioning of French goods and foodstuffs.

CHAPTER FOURTEEN

Into Unoccupied France

*I*t was mid-morning when we arrived in Besançon. We headed down from the station into the beautiful, old part of town, enclosed by the hills and the loop of the river. Up the road to our right was the Caserne Vauban. I could feel its presence behind us. It was so strange to be back. I had seen the town so often from afar but I had never actually been in it before. The whole perspective and feel of the buildings changed from the desirable little toytown I had looked down upon for months to a real, breathing place. We quickly became lost.

'We need to find someone to ask the way,' Frida said, as we stopped by the *mairie*. 'I've got the dentist's address but have no idea how to get there.'

The town seemed to be deserted. What was going on? I saw a sprucely dressed family coming towards us.

'It's Sunday, of course. Everyone's off to church.'

'Oh God, that means we have a full day and night to kill before we can make contact,' replied Frida. 'I only have the man's work address. What are we going to do? We can't stay on the streets.'

'No. And we can't risk another hotel.'

We wandered gloomily around the town for what seemed like hours. By now we were both starving. Buying food proved difficult: although we had money we didn't have any food coupons.[5] Eventually we found a small shop in an alley where we could buy some pears and salt fish. We carried this banquet to a nearby church. We hoped to find, as in Épinal, a quiet side-chapel in which to eat. But on the door of the church was a notice: 'Reservée pour la Wehrmacht'. We stared at it fascinated. We hadn't come across this godly aspect of the invasion before.

We reached a small park and sat on a bench in the cold. Our behaviour brought such strange stares from the warmly clad inhabitants of the town who passed by that we hurried away. In the end we found a deserted municipal washroom and gulped down the food. Two women came in, so we hastily pretended to wash our hands and left. We walked aimlessly around the town. Most of the shops were boarded up for the day. We earmarked a battered hut in what looked like a building site as our quarters for the night. Meanwhile there were still some hours ahead of us. We passed a theatre ablaze with light. The notices outside announced that *La Traviata* was being performed. It had just begun.

'Come on,' I turned to Frida. 'This will keep us off the streets for a few hours.'

I bought two tickets for the gallery and we climbed the stairs. The singing was indifferent but it kept our attention and at least the place was warm. As the curtain went down for the interval I leant over the balcony railings to find a sea of green uniforms below clapping enthusiastically. I shuddered and made a motion downwards to Frida with my eyes, but she was not paying any attention to me.

'Spanish,' she whispered and jerked her head behind.

I turned round cautiously. Sitting behind us was a small group of men talking in rapid Spanish, punctuated by loud laughter. To their delight Frida began to talk to them. They told her that they were Republican soldiers from the recent Spanish Civil War. They had fled the country as refugees and had been herded into French labour camps. Now they were being made to work for the Germans as well but were occasionally allowed Sunday evenings off.

Frida told them, in turn, that she had volunteered for their side during the war and had spent a year working for a radio station and driving an ambulance in Madrid. She also explained our plight. They immediately offered us a bed for the night. This was not only generous but also very brave. If caught they would almost certainly have been shot for harbouring escaped prisoners.

After the performance we followed them to a small room in a run-down building near the river. They told us that they stayed here whenever they could get permission to leave the labour camp. The offer of a bed turned out to be just that: one enormous bed in which they all slept and around which they kept their bicycles. The room was heated by a large stove and soon became warm and stuffy. We greedily shared their fatty sausages and stale bread, which we washed down with a huge casket of rough, red wine.

I crawled over the bicycles and curled up on the bed, exhausted after two nights of very little sleep. I felt safe and warm. In a few minutes I was out. I woke up a couple of times to hear Frida still talking to them, as indomitable as ever. She told me later that they had discussed the Spanish situation until dawn. My last memory of that night is of one of the men hitting the seat of a bicycle shouting 'Muerte a Franco!'

The next morning our Spanish friends gave us directions to the dentist's address. We left them early to be at the surgery as soon as it opened. I told the rather frosty receptionist that I was in agony from a back tooth. We were in luck: there were no other patients yet and we were ushered straight in.

The dentist was an extraordinarily fat man of about sixty with a glistening, bald head and a stony face. He beckoned me to the chair without saying a word. Frida and I were both incredibly nervous. After all, we didn't know for sure that he was even on our side, let alone willing or able to help us.

'Monsieur Bedaux recommended you to us,' said Frida quietly as he peered into my mouth.

'That was very good of him,' he said, with the first hint of warmth coming to his face. 'I hope that I can be of assistance.' He took some francs from his pocket and gave them to me. 'Pay Madame Chaillet on your way out. Be back here at seven o'clock precisely.'

We left. There was another whole day to kill and nothing to do, but we felt elated. Suddenly we were no longer alone. We spent that cold day sheltering in the municipal washroom, having to leave it every time someone came in. We were starving but didn't dare risk another shop. We made do with some bread from the night before.

That evening we approached the surgery at the appointed time. The door was opened by the dentist just as I was raising my hand to ring the bell. He made a small movement with his index finger to indicate silence and led us upstairs. It was obvious that he lived above the surgery. We had had his home address all the time without knowing it! There were four men in the sitting room. They rose as one when we entered.

'Messieurs,' he said with a flourish of his hand. 'May I present our brave young Englishwomen.'

Formal introductions were made. Our companions turned out to be the mayor of the town, a schoolmaster, a lawyer and the owner of a bicycle shop. They questioned us closely about conditions in both camps. They were particularly interested in the security arrangements at Vittel and seemed pleased and even amused at the idea of a hole in the perimeter wire there. They also wanted information on suspected German collaborators among the French workmen at both camps, but we had no hard evidence to give them, just a few rumours that the lawyer carefully wrote down. The helpfulness of our heating engineer and his friend was also noted.

Suddenly all discussion was at an end. The dentist went to the kitchen and returned with a tray bearing two bottles of wine and the wonderful sight of green olives! He filled our glasses. We raised them and all stood. It was the mayor who spoke.

'To General de Gaulle, Monsieur Churchill and our new friends here.'

We drank the toast and then huddled around the radio set while the schoolmaster fiddled with the dials to get the BBC news from London. At last Stuart Hibberd came over loud and clear. 'Good evening,' he said. I could picture him there in his dinner jacket and I found myself saying 'Good evening' back to him in my shabby clothes and broken shoes. I looked at Frida. We both had tears in our eyes.

We stayed that night in the attic room above the bicycle shop. It was in a small courtyard off the rue de la Vieille Monnaie, a quiet street at the far end of town. Like so many of these courtyards in Besançon, it was reached through an imposing main door that led off the street. I felt secure and hidden in this little warren of old buildings. For the whole of the following day we sat quietly on our bed. I found a copy of Balzac's *Les Paysans* on a bookshelf in the room. I spent the time reading it, relishing his descriptions of the wily French peasants.

The real surprise for us came that evening. It was Armistice Day – 11 November. The whole town seemed to be out celebrating, regardless of the German army's presence. It was their way of showing defiance. We were taken to a cavernous old bar on the way up to the citadel at the far end of town. There we were introduced to everyone and feted for being British escapees. The wine and the cognac quickly went to our heads as this was the first serious drinking we had done in months.

We were then led through the back door to a very elegant photographic studio where an elderly man silently took our photos for new identity papers. This done, the dentist insisted on taking us to another bar in the town centre, full of *anciens combattants* (veterans). No introductions were made this time, perhaps due to the presence of some young German soldiers drinking at the far end. Frida and

I became increasingly nervous as the endless toasts were made – to victory, de Gaulle, revenge, Churchill and (curiously) the Labour politician Stafford Cripps. When the veterans started on a gutsy rendition of 'La Marseillaise' we pleaded tiredness and asked our friend to take us home.

'I think we're going to make it, Frida,' I said as we lay on our beds later that night. 'We're going to get real help. Thank goodness your contact was sound. I was so scared but I can almost see the Swiss border now, we're so close.'

'Perhaps we'll be dining in a flashy Zurich restaurant on Saturday night,' she said with a smile. 'The Hoffmans will be surprised when we turn up on their doorstep!'

Carl Hoffman was an old friend of her father's from Cambridge. We were relying on him to make arrangements for our return to England.

The next day passed in a whirl as the news of our presence quickly spread around the town. Everyone seemed to want to greet us and to share their paltry rations. We even tasted real coffee for the first time in well over a year. It was made proudly for us by the owner of a large hotel. That evening the dentist and the mayor produced our false identity cards, ration books, food coupons and an extra 500 francs (about £120 today). I was identified as an Anna Triolet, aged twenty-two, originally from Avignon.

'These documents are fine but not so good that they'd stand up to much more than a quick examination,' said the mayor as we went over them.

'That doesn't matter too much. If you're searched they're bound to find your British passports,' the dentist added in a matter-of-fact way. 'Have you taken off all the labels from your English clothes?'

We nodded. My clothes could pass as French (thanks to Madame Manguin) but I was concerned that Frida's looked very English.

The bicycle shop owner woke us very early the next morning. He led us wordlessly in the dark through a maze of streets to a small courtyard where he ushered us onto the back of a horse-drawn wagon. He kissed us goodbye. The wagon pulled off while it was still dark. After what seemed an interminable ride we reached a small village where we were put onto the back of an old lorry. A couple of hours later we stopped at the rear entrance of a hotel. We were now very near the Swiss border. A nervous young woman carrying a baby in her arms led us into the dining room. While we ate a meal of stale bread and hot milk she told us that she was the manageress. Her husband was a soldier who had been captured in May 1940. She had heard that he was imprisoned in Germany but didn't know where.

'You will remain in here', she said, showing us into a back room. 'If the front door bell rings you must hide in the wardrobe. I will lock it and take the key.' She saw the look of dismay on our faces.

'I am sorry, but this is necessary,' she added. 'The contact who'll be bringing you over the border won't be here until tonight.' She hurried back to her duties elsewhere.

It was a long, boring day stuck in that back room with nothing to do and no books to read. We spent a few uncomfortable and suffocating periods locked in the wardrobe keeping absolutely silent. We were pent-up with excitement and expectation, for the Swiss border and freedom seemed almost within touching distance. That evening our contact was brought to see us. He was a tall, thin man who could not have been much older than I was. He paced the room nervously and could hardly look us in the eyes as he told us the news.

'The main problem in getting you out of France is that this whole area on both sides is heavily policed by German, French and Swiss guards,' he began. 'Last week a *passeur* took three escaping English soldiers over. One fell and twisted his ankle. The others carried him but they were all caught, including my compatriot. We have no news of him yet.'

'How much will it cost?' asked Frida, cutting straight to the point, as ever. She'd realized what the man's nerves were about. 'We've got money to pay.'

'There is perhaps someone who will take you over. But it will cost 10,000 francs,' he replied, turning his head away.

We stared at him, open mouthed. 'But that's robbery!' I shouted. 'We've only got about 1,000 francs between us. You can have it all.'

'That's not enough.'

'You've got to help us. We've escaped from a camp and just want to get home. We're not tourists. We can't go back. You can have all the money we've got.'

'This is war, Mademoiselle, not one of your cricket matches.' And with that rather fatuous reply he stormed out. The young woman looked at us apologetically.

'I shall arrange for you to return to Besançon as soon as possible,' she said and left the room.

We were shocked. We had come so far and were now only a few miles from freedom. I sat on the bed, stunned. Frida took charge of the situation.

'We've got to change our plans, Pat. We'll go over the line into the Unoccupied Zone and then down to Marseille. We can get a boat from there.'

'How do you know? You're just guessing. It'll be just as difficult to get across the line. They might want even more money.'

'No. I've heard it's not as bad as the Swiss border. There are only a few German sentries on bicycles with guard dogs. And that's for a border hundreds of miles long. Come on, it's the only thing left for us.'

The hotel manageress was as good as her word. We were taken back to Besançon in a decrepit lorry later that evening and spent a rather miserable night above the bicycle shop. By dawn we were on our way south again to a village called Arbois on the demarcation line. To our amazement we were driven there in an official police car. 'Vive le BBC!' were the policeman's parting words as he left us at a farmhouse.

The old couple there led us into the kitchen and then left us alone. They had their own work to do in the fields. We were learning fast that people who helped us had to keep up the routine of their normal lives, to hide the huge risks they were taking. This often meant that they hardly spoke to us, if at all. As it got dark the couple came back from the fields. We all sat by the fire in silence, waiting for the guide that the policeman had promised us. When he finally arrived he turned out to be a rather pimply boy of no more than about fifteen.

'200 francs each,' he quickly told us. 'And don't make a sound. We'll be there in a few hours.'

The old lady gave us some bread, which we put into our pockets. We followed him out. He seemed very unconcerned. I got the impression that he did this trip regularly. Well, if that was the case it was easier for him than it was for me.

We had only a few miles of the wooded, boggy country to cross but it was rough going. It was a moonlit night and very cold. We could hear the dogs baying far away; I shivered at the thought of being savaged by an Alsatian. At one point I sank into a bog. The boy pulled me clear and put his hand deep into the squelchy mud to retrieve my rather sorry-looking boot.

The crossing was a nightmare: the swamps, the cold, the fearsome noise of the dogs in the darkness and the thought of being shot by a German guard. And all the time we were pushing though thick woodland with the branches catching in our clothes. There was no track and I was terrified that the boy would go too fast and leave us in this dark wood. Not once did he look round to see if we were following and we didn't dare get too close in case the branches that he was pushing through came swinging back into our faces.

He stopped. 'Keep quiet and stay here. I have to do something for my father. I'll be back soon.' With that he was gone.

Frida and I looked at each other in horror. I reached out and took her hand. I didn't want to be left alone. All I could hear was the noise of the dogs at the other side of the wood. There is something so primeval about that sound; perhaps it's the instinctive terror of the hunted. I don't know what we would have done if it had gone on much longer. Probably fled back through the bog to light and people. The boy suddenly reappeared, just as quietly as he had left. Without a word he simply started walking again, with Frida and I stumbling along behind. Suddenly he turned to us as we approached a river.

'We're near the line now,' he whispered. 'Be absolutely quiet. If I hear a sentry I will run. Be ready. Here, hold my hand.'

We crept out from the wood to the small track used by the soldiers. There was no one about. We moved slowly down to a little bridge and were met by a friend of his who was about the same age.

'You're in the *zone libre*,' he said by way of greeting.

'Vive la France!' Frida shouted as we hugged each other. 'We've made it.'

'Quiet! The Germans will still shoot if they see you.' Our guide put his finger to his lips in alarm.

The boys took us to a farmhouse near by where their bicycles were propped up outside. We sat on the crossbars clutching our bags. It was like being the figurehead on a battering ram: they simply took their feet off the pedals and freewheeled at a terrifying speed down the steep hill to the village of Poligny. We stopped at the back of an inn where our guide knocked at the door. A man came out and nodded in our direction. Not a word was said by anyone. Our guides seemed to melt away before we could even thank them.

The proprietor's wife led us into the kitchen. She was a friendly, motherly woman of about fifty. Over a meal of hot bean broth she began to explain about life on this side of the demarcation line.

'Be careful,' she warned us. 'Where you have just come from you can see your enemy in their uniforms and everyone knows the collaborators. Here it is different. The Germans don't wear their uniforms and in Vichy France everyone suspects his neighbour. If you have to speak at all, speak in French.'

We had dried off by now and felt much warmer. She took a candle and showed us up the stairs. At the top she halted and turned round to look at us.

'We have to go through another room to get to your bedroom,' she said. 'It is occupied by the sister of a policeman. She will report you if she hears you speaking English. Just so that you know.'

We were past caring. I was so tired that I curled up on the bed and went to sleep without a word. The next morning we were up late. Thankfully, our neighbour in the next room had gone. Sitting downstairs in the warm kitchen we told the family about our escape. We were among friends. Henri, the proprietor, was a soulful looking man who had been badly wounded at Verdun in 1916. He took out a bottle of brandy and toasted us. I drank it happily even though it was not yet midday.

'Tell them in London,' he said, 'that not all of France has given in to the Germans.'

As he couldn't organize a lift for us to Lyon until the next day, we spent that afternoon with his older daughter, a rabidly anti-German girl of about twenty. She proudly took us to meet her friends. Perhaps this was not the wisest thing to do but she was terribly eager to show us off. Talking to them we began to understand how the age-old animosity between the north and south of the country had been inflamed by the new division imposed by the Germans. Rumours of the behaviour on either side of this fortified line were cleverly circulated to build up jealousy and despair. They also told us of the intrigue and double-dealing that went on in Vichy France.

'Sometimes people just disappear,' a rather serious girl told us.

I was amazed. 'But surely you know what's happened and why? I mean, you must see them leaving their homes with the German soldiers?'

She shook her head. 'You won't see many German soldiers around here. It's the *gendarmes* who do the dirty work. I saw them hustle our neighbour into a car.'

'Something similar happened to me in Paris,' I said.

'Yes,' she replied. 'But you weren't on the German list simply because someone hated you.'

This group of friends were desperate to help us get away. We were touched by the enthusiasm of everyone that we met on our first day in Unoccupied France. Indeed, we had had nothing but help in both zones over the past few days. Our journey from Besançon up to the Swiss border, back again and now over the demarcation line had been organized by a network of people who had risked a great deal for us. No one seemed to ask just who these English girls who needed help were. After all, we could easily have been spies or informers, yet people didn't hesitate to help us.

This spirit of self-sacrifice and bravery was very different to the widespread image of French collapse and cowardice that we encountered when we got back to London. Frida and I were to travel all over Britain in the months that followed our return, giving talks about our experiences. I see from my notes for one of them that I said, 'Thanks to the French people who sheltered us, fed us and gave us money at the risk of their lives we made our way . . . ' That was no exaggeration.

Early the following day a silk merchant drove us to Lyon while we sang our hearts out in the safe confines of a big car jogging hesitantly along on poor petrol. We were heading for the US Consulate. As in Paris, this still-neutral country had a British Interests Section attached to its diplomatic mission. It was our intention to see if we could get some sort of protection from the US authorities to travel on the Paris-Lyon-

Marseille express. Our driver dropped us on the outskirts of the city, as he was heading off elsewhere. He told us that even though it was Sunday the concierge at the Consulate would be around; he could help us with somewhere to stay for the night. We set off into town. It was a long walk and it wasn't until early afternoon that we finally got to the Consulate. We found it completely shut up with no sign of anyone, let alone a concierge. We looked at each other in despair.

'We can't wander around yet another town until tomorrow,' I said. 'Our luck is only going to take us so far.'

'Well, we don't have any choice. Come on, let's see Lyon and then decide what to do.'

It felt so odd walking around looking at shops with goods on display in the windows and to see people bustling about. The absence of German uniforms and posters on the streets was strange. We both felt a little overwhelmed and took refuge in a cinema. We saw a dreadful film on the life of Beethoven. It was one of those soupy hagiographies where Beethoven kept gazing out of the window looking constipated while music rose around him. We didn't care. At least it put off the moment of having to make a decision.

'Pat,' Frida whispered as the film swelled to its finish. 'I don't think we can wait. Our papers aren't good enough to risk in a strange hotel and I'm nervous here. We don't know anything about this city.'

'I agree. Let's just take our chances on the train to Marseille.'

'Fine,' Frida said after some hesitation. 'Somehow or other we'll contact the US Consul once we're there. At least we'll be on the coast and not stuck in the middle of France.'

We were both worried and frightened about getting the train without official US help. Henri in Poligny had told us that the train could be heavily patrolled as it came from Paris and crossed the demarcation line. But what else could we do? Maybe we were influenced by the previous afternoon's talk but Lyon definitely felt different from Besançon and Nancy. It was full of elegant buildings and busy streets, yet was curiously oppressive. We had had such high hopes when crossing the line but now we just wanted to get away. We picked up our bags and went straight to the station, which was as beautiful, impressive and dangerous as the rest of the city.

It was a nerve-racking journey. The train lurched and shuddered its way down to Marseille. At any moment we expected to hear the order 'Vos papiers, s'il vous plaît.' It never came. I don't know if the atmosphere was a projection of our own fears, but the whole train felt tense and worried. People were quiet or talking in whispers. They seemed to be waiting for something or perhaps someone to come and demand what everyone was doing there. No one came, nothing happened. Slowly, slowly we pulled into Marseille.

And then we realized why the train had been empty of officials. An inspection was indeed going to take place, but much more thoroughly and much more slowly at the ticket barrier. As we disembarked we could see a group of officials ahead, carefully checking the passengers' papers. The beginning of a long queue was forming. We joined it, not looking at each other, knowing that this was the end. There was no way our papers were going to fool this sort of official check.

The train had pulled in at an end platform. Looking around in despair we saw a wall of railway buildings along the side of the platform. They had the usual drab, dusty look which makes them merge into one long, unidentifiable building. Amazingly, we caught sight of a sign marked 'Hôtel' above a door. Unnoticed in the large, noisy queue we pushed open the door and found ourselves in the station restaurant. Another sign pointed to a long passage. We followed it and found ourselves in a different world. We were in a foyer with all the activity and comfort of a forgotten era: the Hôtel Terminus.

Our luck had held after all. We had arrived unscathed in Marseille.

CHAPTER FIFTEEN

Settling Down in Marseille

For a few moments we simply stood there, dazed but relieved to have got away from the police check. We were bewildered by the luxury that confronted us. It was obvious that we were vulnerable: with our battered bags and shabby clothes we stood out a mile. Would our false papers be good enough here? Could we even afford to pay for a room?

'Let's try him,' Frida said suddenly, pointing towards a man reading *The New York Times*. Before I could say anything she had approached him.

'I'm sorry to bother you,' she said in her most polite Cambridge accent. 'But we need to get in contact with the US Consul urgently. Could you possibly help us?'

'I take it you're English?' he asked quietly, looking around him. 'Why don't you sit down and tell me a bit about yourselves.'

I quickly took him through as much of our story as I wanted him to know. I admitted we had crossed into Vichy France without proper papers but carefully said nothing about escaping from Vittel. He listened thoughtfully.

'Well, your luck is still holding,' he said when I'd finished. 'You could have asked anyone in this lobby but you chose me and I know the Vice-Consul. I'll see if I can get him at home on the telephone. You wait here.'

We couldn't quite believe this. Since getting off the train a few minutes before it seemed that we couldn't do anything wrong. He went up to the desk and made a very quick call, returning to where we were sitting with a broad smile on his face.

'Mr Randall is speaking to the people here at the hotel to see if you can be put up for the night. You're to be at his office at ten o'clock tomorrow morning. Here's the address,' he said, writing something in his pocketbook and tearing out a sheet.

He escorted us to the front desk where a pompous man visibly shivered with disapproval as we handed him our passports. He gave us our key but offered no help in getting to our room.

'I don't know how to thank you,' I said to our American helper. 'We don't even know your name.'

'John Powers. And no need to thank me. Look, I was stationed in Hampshire during the last war. And we're soon going to be in this one together. I only wish I could do more to help you but I'm not staying in town. Mr Randall will look after you. He's a good man.'

As we went in search of our room, Mr Powers returned to his chair and the perusal of his newspaper. It had been an extraordinary chance meeting. We didn't even know what he was doing in the hotel.

Our overnight stay was scarcely a hardship for the room was truly luxurious. The bathroom had soap, wonderful large towels, hot water and a bathmat. I found some bath salts and spent most of the evening wallowing in bliss while Frida lay fretting on her bed.

We were at the US Consulate just before ten the next morning. There was quite a crowd of people waiting there. Much to our surprise we were ushered into a small anteroom which had a table and chairs. A large man entered and sat down in front of us. He was smoking a pipe and was in his shirtsleeves. For some irrelevant reason, I noted to myself that a British consular official would never have taken off his jacket while at work.

'Lee J. Randall, Vice-Consul,' he said, shaking our hands. 'Pleased to make your acquaintance. And your names are?'

'Rosemary Say and Frida Stewart,' I replied. 'We've escaped from the British Womens' Camp at Vittel and want to return to England.'

I quickly told our story and he made some notes on a pad, asking a few questions. His manner was friendly, even fatherly, but also businesslike.

'The first thing to understand,' he said when I had finished, 'is that I can't wave a magic wand and return you home. This city is the gateway out of Europe. It's flooded with refugees from all over. Walk downtown and you'll meet Poles, Belgians, Czechs and others from every walk of life. Some have money while others are destitute. But they all have one thing on their mind: escape. To the USA, Canada, England, wherever.'

'But you can help with the paperwork for us to get back home?' I interrupted in a worried voice.

'Yes, Miss Say, we can certainly do that. You'll need permission to leave France and also visas for transit through both Spain and Portugal. Once you're in Lisbon we'll get you home by boat or plane. The British Interests Section here will help with money, ration cards and food coupons. You'll need to register yourselves with the police. But don't forget that you're going to be sitting a very long time on the quayside.'

We both must have looked extremely puzzled at this last sentence. Mr Randall raised his palms to us and smiled.

'I didn't mean to be flippant,' he continued, 'but you need to come to terms with the fact that it may take months to get the paperwork done. Everyone is after the same thing.'

'But we're not,' I said in slight desperation. 'We simply want to get home. We're not refugees trying to get into a foreign country.'

'Yes, there is that distinction but it doesn't make much of a difference, Miss Say. Transit visas for anyone are still difficult to come by. The Spaniards aren't that keen on refugees from France flooding into their country. They can hardly feed their own people as it is. The border is constantly being closed. The same goes for the Portuguese. Plus, the Vichy bureaucracy here can't cope with the numbers needing papers. Marseille is full. There's hardly a room to be had in the hotels.'

Mr Randall certainly knew how to let us down. We had naïvely assumed that with American help our visas would come through in a matter of days. He considered us for a few moments.

'Look, I can get you a room at Madame Morbelli's,' he said somewhat reluctantly. 'But no complaints. She's on the rue Saint-Victoire. Appropriate maybe?' he said smiling. He quickly scribbled down the address and got up to go.

'I'm sure you'll want to contact your parents. Come next door to my secretary's room. She'll arrange money and coupons. She'll also do you a letter giving you permission to be out after curfew.'

We were both allowed to send telegrams home of strictly fifteen words (plus name). Mine read:

ARRIVED HERE SAFELY AWAITING REPATRIATION VIA LISBON THROUGH AMERICAN CONSUL MARSEILLES HOPE ARRIVE HOME JANUARY. ROSEMARY SAY.

When I eventually reached London I discovered that this brief telegram had totally bewildered my poor parents. They thought (quite naturally) that I was still at the camp in Vittel! What were we doing in Marseille? Neither Frida nor I had thought about this when we sent messages to our loved ones. My father contacted the Prisoner of War Department at the Foreign Office the same day he received my telegram. Although this was 'unexpected but excellent news,' he wrote, 'we cannot imagine why these two girls are suddenly being repatriated. We have not heard that either has been ill. We can hardly think that they have escaped. We hope their present position is secure and safe.' To my parents it all sounded like the typical muddle of their younger daughter.

This was, in fact, the beginning of a constant exchange of letters and telegrams between my father and various British Government departments over the following months as we attempted to make our way back to England.

Looking through this sheaf of documents many years later I was struck by the constant demands for money made by the British government to my father. He replied to our telegram with one of his own and for this privilege he was charged the enormous sum of £1.7s.4d. (well over £50 in today's money). I have no idea what would have happened if he couldn't have paid; as it was, the total cost of getting us home was to be a serious concern for him. The demand for the telegram payment was typical of the bureaucracy of the time. My father received a bill that had been typed and copied. He then had to pay and was given two signed and stamped receipts.

Through Mr Randall's office I was able to send a letter to my parents a few days later. It was remarkably clichéd. Perhaps I was just too anxious to reassure my family that I would get home and that I was well cared for and safe. I wrote: 'So I shall soon be home – a prodigal daughter who has gone through the most extraordinary experiences. I am having a real holiday here and the weather is gorgeous.' I realized just how much I wanted and needed to hear from my family when Frida received a reply to her telegram a week before I did. I was very jealous and told my parents so in no uncertain terms in my next letter.

Mr Randall's offer of Madame Morbelli's hotel sounded fine to us. It was in a quiet side street in the centre of town, next to a beautiful church. And this ample lady was indeed fine, with her red-tinted hair and make-up of purple, blue, green and cerise. She reminded me of the madam from Boulogne in the Besançon camp. She put us in a large, bright and sparsely furnished room overlooking the street. There was only one drawback.

'One of my gentlemen is a commercial traveller,' she explained as she adjusted her corsage. 'He sometimes comes back for one thing or another and always uses this room. So I am afraid, my dears, that when he does you will have to stay with my friend Marie-Ange. But don't worry,' she continued as she saw the looks of dismay on our faces, 'It's better than sleeping on the Vieux Port. And she is always most careful to change the sheets.'

Madame Morbelli obviously had a beady eye for business but she was as good as her word. She ran a truly bourgeois establishment. Our impeccably starched sheets were kept neatly folded in a box at the foot of the bed when we had to vacate the room. During the few months that we stayed there we hardly ever saw anybody in the building and certainly never heard any movement. It was very unlike my idea of a brothel. I found, to my great delight, a leather-bound collection of French classics in a glass cabinet downstairs and would contentedly spend hours reading. Our few visits to Marie-Ange were slightly less comfortable, as we were expected to stay away from our room for long periods of the day and evening.

Madame Morbelli was anxious that we go to the prefecture of police as soon as possible to establish our legal identity. She warned us that although this might be the Unoccupied Zone there were still constant police round-ups and random checks at hotels and cafes. Accordingly, we joined a huge queue of anxious refugees on our second day with her. It was shocking to see just how many people had been displaced by the war. We were all waiting our turn to be accepted as temporary residents in this already overflowing city. Desperate and frightened people clamoured and pushed to get through and obtain their precious papers. Scuffles broke out as the day wore on. Occasionally people would emerge from the building shouting and protesting at their treatment inside. A man behind us in the queue kept up a constant, depressing conversation.

'Nobody can influence the decisions of Monsieur le Préfet, of course, but then he wants no trouble with his masters,' was his constant theme. 'He can send us all back where we came from.'

He told us his life story a number of times, always ending with the question, 'And where do you come from?'

We let him continue with his depressing talk but told him nothing about ourselves. I was getting worried that we might be sent straight back to Vittel. Just as dusk came we were taken in to see a young official. We had decided the previous night that we would tell the authorities everything and hope for the best. He silently took a few notes then asked for our passports. To our great surprise he quickly signed and stamped some pieces of paper with a great flourish.

'I have no wish to make things difficult for our English *mesdemoiselles*,' he said as he handed them to us with our passports. He gave a broad smile. 'May I wish you a pleasant stay in our beautiful city,' he continued, seemingly without a hint of irony.

The evening was wet and raw as we made our way back to Madame Morbelli's. We were feeling on top of the world. Our luck had held. We had somewhere to stay, food cards and even the blessing of a Vichy official who liked England! Our worried parents had been informed of our whereabouts. We had officially joined the recognized army of people hoping to start their lives elsewhere. We were not leaving home, however, but going back to it. All we had to do now was wait.

CHAPTER SIXTEEN

The Wait

For the first few days in Marseille we could hardly bear to leave our room. We had been so frightened and physically exhausted that it was enough just to sit quietly on the bed reading. Life gradually settled into a routine. Every week we went along to see Mr Randall who gave us an allowance to pay our way (this money was to be added to our debt to the British Government when we returned to England). Once we recovered our confidence, Frida and I began to go our separate ways. Perhaps this was no bad thing. Our dependence on each other and our common trust had kept us going through some pretty difficult times. Our friendship held fast, but in everyday life we often found quite different diversions and interests.

Frida, of course, was of a serious political mind: she wanted to know what the local people were thinking and doing. As always, she seemed to talk to everyone. She found that many listened illegally to the BBC rather than to the Vichy-controlled radio stations and that they bought Swiss or underground newspapers when they could. She came back one afternoon with a wonderfully acid comment from a schoolteacher on Vichy newspapers: 'I don't use them even to wrap my boots in. They're not strong enough.' Clandestine papers such as *La Marseillaise* had circulations far larger than the number of copies actually printed, since each edition was read by numerous people. In this way it seemed that in spite of the strict censorship, everyone knew about the strikes and sabotage acts that were going on in railway yards and factories in the Unoccupied Zone. Details of reprisal shootings by the authorities also seemed to be common knowledge.

Frida encountered much grumbling about the amount of local products that disappeared to Germany, including the famous *savon de Marseille*. But it was the lack of petrol that seemed to cause the most resentment, as this hit the fishing trade which was the city's main industry. Perhaps surprisingly, she didn't find much evidence that the British blockade on food entering the port was producing anti-British feeling. According to what she told me, the people understood the need to stop imported food being diverted to Germany and the German army. 'C'est naturel' was the way they justified it over and over again.

In fact, the food shortages here were far worse than the rationing we were to experience when we got home to England. Conditions in Marseille were so appalling that they made even our diet in the camps seem generous. The lack of food dominated our lives. Bread was severely rationed and often not available. You could queue for hours outside a shop, often on a mere rumour, only to find that there was nothing left. Tuberculosis was rife. It was shocking to see emaciated children with bloated stomachs wandering the streets of the city. The staple food seemed to consist principally of carrots disguised in different ways. Some years later, Frida described a typical restaurant menu:

Potage Paysanne (carrots and water)
Filet de Boeuf Garni (carrots plus a small scrap of meat)
Macedoine de Legumes (mainly carrots)
Carrottes Vichy

The city was a fascinating mixture of people, intrigues and aspirations. I quickly established my favourite cafe on the Vieux Port. I would bring a book and sit there contentedly from mid-morning onwards drinking worse coffee than I thought could be possible in France (usually burnt acorns and barley) and smoking cigarettes made from dried tea leaves. Frida would arrive at some point in the day but quickly dash off elsewhere. Towards noon the same groups of people would start to stroll in as if they were walking into their front parlours. For the first few days no one took any notice of me. I didn't care. I was in a cocoon of my own world.

One afternoon a short, slight man approached my table. He bowed slightly, stood very correctly before me and spoke in halting French.

'May I introduce myself, Mademoiselle? I am Alfred Ziege, from Frankfurt. We have heard you are English. Would you care to join us?' He pointed to a small group at the far side of the cafe.

'Thank you, I'd love to.' I walked over to their table. 'My name is Rosemary Say. But everyone calls me Pat.'

'Pat, this is Fritz who lives in the same building as me. He's also German. And this is Jean and Marek.'

A languid arm stretched across to give me a handshake and a strong Belgian accent welcomed me into the group. I smiled. Then suddenly my hand was seized and a wonderfully overblown, romantic kiss was placed neatly in the middle of my palm by the other man.

'Welcome. I am Marek.' He pointed at me. 'We did not know what to make of you and your friend. Two nice English girls sitting in a cafe. You seemed the most unlikely spies.'

He was looking at me and laughing as I began to stammer out explanations and credentials. He was a very good-looking man with sharp features, a precise moustache and a thick mop of reddish, wavy hair which sat high on his head. His eyes were intelligent yet dreamy. He knew exactly what effect he was having on me.

'Don't worry, you've been well spoken of,' he teased.

They accepted me into their group. We spent the next couple of hours sitting there and telling our life stories. They were all penniless refugees who used the cafe as a club, as they waited (like me) for visas to get away from Marseille.

By the end of the day I was deeply in love with Marek. He was a Polish Jew who had spent a number of years in France where he seemed to have made a good living as a writer, poet and literary critic. He had family in the USA and was waiting for a boat to join them. Up to that point my late-adolescent romances had been given a sadly disappointing run. At seventeen I had defiantly lost my virginity in a Folkestone hotel to the captain of a French cross-Channel steamer. There had been the brief and rather anonymous moments with the young soldier on the train from Avignon and the Toulouse police officer in Paris who had promised to send a letter to my parents. My other romances had been rather chaste affairs. But now I knew better.

In the following few weeks Marek and I would spend hours discussing the state of mankind. He would make me sit absolutely still while he read Stendhal out loud. He could have read the Bible to me in Hebrew and I would have been just as enchanted. I was amused by his serious concern that he might not like the American way of life. He had seen just one Hollywood film and had hated it.

'What poetry and culture is going to come out of cowboys and Indians?' he demanded one afternoon.

We were sitting in opposite chairs at the cafe. With his love of drama he had taken my hands and sunk his chin in them, staring into my eyes. I was delighted by the attention and the theatricality of the gesture.

'You don't need to be too concerned,' I teased in return. 'I think America's a big enough place for you to fit in somewhere.'

I learnt years later how common this fear of the unknown was among many would-be refugees. The Jewish artist Marc Chagall, for example, was very reluctant to accept that his French citizenship might not save him from imprisonment by the Germans. He left the country in 1941, only after he had been reassured that there were, in fact, cows in America!

Marek accepted my adoration with good grace. He would take me to bed when Frida had gone out for the day. Madame Morbelli looked after us indulgently. Perhaps she was more accustomed to commercial love and found that my starry eyed happiness made a nice change. It is only in retrospect that I can see how ours was a typical wartime romance. At no point was it suggested that I try to get to the USA or he to England. And as time went on my main worry (seemingly without any guilt) was that he would find his boat before I left. So much for the largesse of love.

Alfred also became a firm friend after our first meeting. He was a dedicated Communist who had fled Germany in the mid-1930s. He was a tailor by profession and lived in a tiny room, most of which was taken up by a sewing machine. He seemed to make a living of sorts, even though we could never work out how.

He became my constant companion at the cinema, which was another cheap way of passing the time. While some films were enjoyable, the shorts that accompanied them were hard to bear. They were sickly stuff, even by Vichy standards, based on Marshal Pétain's pathetic tag of *Travail, Famille, Patrie* (Work, Family, Country). One I remember was about a young man learning the folly of his ways in the big city, only to return to the loving bosom of his family who forgave him everything. The one consolation for having to sit through such drivel was to see the 'Vive de Gaulle!' slogans that had been daubed on the cinema walls under the cover of darkness.

'Pat, you must teach me English,' Alfred said one day as he sat at his machine mending my battered coat. 'I have decided I want to go and live in Canada.'

And so began his abortive attempt to learn the language. We started with really simple things, given that he had hardly a word of English.

He would sit at his machine in the evening concentrating on his pronunciation and sewing while I perched on his small bed listing elementary phrases and correcting him. Most evenings our lesson would be interrupted by Fritz who was standing and listening at the open door. He would at some point take exception to a word that Alfred was trying to learn and say something to him in German. This would then start a fierce argument between them. Fritz had been a member of the Social Democratic Party. As such he was prepared to blame the Communist Party, in the guise of Alfred, almost single-handedly for the rise of the Nazis. Alfred would reply in kind.

Sometimes they would be joined in argument by other German friends, one noisy anarchist in particular. Almost always the discussion was about the past. This was old-time European politics, ready to defend lost causes that had little to do with today's problems. As with many others we met, discussion was all. There was the past and (sometimes) the future, but the present did not seem to be important. They were indomitable.

Like all the other refugee groups, we marked out our tables every day at the Vieux Port cafe. The proprietor resignedly accepted the fact that all he could expect by way of custom from us was perhaps a couple of cups of coffee among eight to ten people, most of whom appropriated his chess sets.

Looking back at my friends during those months in Marseille, it is impossible to say that we were in any way a really close group. There was a lot of suspicion and hopelessness amongst all of us. Feelings ran high and quarrels were loud and violent. We all shared the worry of uncertainty: exactly when would we get away? And just about everyone apart from Frida and myself faced the question of where they would go and what they would do when they got there. We all took comfort, however, from the sheer numbers of people who wanted to leave. We certainly weren't alone in our predicament.

It was sad to see the waste of intellect and ability as the delays lengthened and the future for many continued to look bleak. Sometimes a friend would not appear at the cafe. Had he got his visa at last, had he been arrested or had he just scarpered into the countryside to try his luck away from the pressures of the city? We waited and wondered. But if the person didn't come back he was soon forgotten. We were only really held together by a common wish to be off and away and to begin our lives again.

As we got into December I began to worry more and more about my two beautiful pigskin suitcases. I had left them at the Izards' in Paris on my arrest. If we were going to be leaving France quite soon, as I desperately hoped, then I wanted to take them with me. They were the smartest possessions I had ever had, excluding the ski suit left behind in the camp. Frida was amused at this concern for my luggage, which had begun to border on the obsessive.

An elderly German man at our table came up with a surprising remark one afternoon, as we were sitting in the cafe and I was again bemoaning the loss of my suitcases.

'Why don't you go to the Thomas Cook office, young lady?' he said in a pinched tone. 'There's one near by. Aren't they supposed to be able to arrange all travel requirements?'

I detected a hint of sarcasm but ignored it. The following day I dragged Frida along to their offices. I briefly explained the situation to a rather effete young clerk who sat behind the desk.

'I'll leave well alone if it means that my friends in Paris are compromised in any way,' I added quickly. 'But I would like to take my luggage on to England. Could you please advise me?'

'That should be no problem, Mademoiselle,' replied the man in a rather bored voice. 'Please fill out these forms. There is a fee of fifty francs. Your luggage should be here within a week and it will be delivered to your address.'

Rather dazed, I completed the formalities and signed the forms. Sitting in a bar later with Frida and having a celebratory drink of coffee, I thought through the whole extraordinary episode.

'The clerk didn't seem particularly surprised at my request, did he?'

'No.' Frida considered the matter. 'I suppose there are lots of people like you who had to leave in a hurry and now want to get their possessions back.'

'Maybe. But there can't be many like me who have been imprisoned and then want to get their luggage back from their place of arrest!'

We both smiled at this. Surprising though it might seem in retrospect, at no time did either of us consider that the whole transaction might be foolhardy. Indeed, it was only after the war that I learnt from Madame Izard how disconcerted she had been to find a messenger at her door one morning with a signed note from me requesting that my luggage be released. She had not heard from me for weeks and had been terribly worried. Now what had happened? Was I not still behind barbed wire at Vittel? She hadn't liked this unexpected demand but had concurred. There was nothing else for her to do.

Some days later my suitcases arrived. Madame Morbelli raised no objection to letting me unpack and store my things in a small back room away from the eyes of the commercial traveller. She had seen the quality of the leather and perhaps imagined that I must have a rich family back home. These suitcases are much too heavy for anyone to use nowadays. They are under my writing desk and still have their battered labels on the side: *Wagons Lits/Cook, 2 Place de la Madeleine, Paris.*

One Monday morning early in December I made my way to our cafe. It was unusually crowded for this time of day and buzzed with excitement. Marek rushed forward and hugged me.

'Pat. The Americans have come into the war!' he cried. 'The Japanese attacked them last night.'

We spent the rest of the day celebrating the American entry and speculating over its significance. One unexpected side effect of their involvement was to make me feel increasingly insecure. What would happen to Mr Randall and the Consulate now that the USA was in the war? Would I still get money? Would anyone be working on my visa? Events were moving too fast and I needed to feel the security of my pre-war world. I began to think about the Manguins in Avignon. I wanted to see them.

I made the decision to visit them on the spur of the moment. We were all talking about our plans for Christmas when I suddenly blurted out, 'I'd like to go to Avignon. To see the Manguin family.'

Everyone looked at me quizzically before Jean led the way in protest in his slightly patronizing drawl. 'Pat, I would strongly advise you not to go. Remember that you are an escaped prisoner of war. You would have to get official permission to travel. Don't bring yourself to the attention of the authorities if you don't need to.'

But it was pointless trying to dissuade me. I was determined to go. It was a year and a half since I had last seen the family and during all that time I had been in a state of constant worry for my future well-being. At this particular moment I just needed the comfort of a familiar, pre-war life with people who loved me. If I could not yet get back to my own family in North London then Madame Odette's in Avignon would be a more than adequate substitute. I later explained this to Frida who understood completely. She agreed to come with me.

The next few days were hectic. With some difficulty I got in touch with the Manguins. I knew that they had moved to the Île de la Barthelasse, a cigar-shaped island in the middle of the Rhône by Avignon's Palais des Papes. In my letter I was at pains to stress to Madame Odette that I wanted to visit only for a couple of days. I assured her that we would come only if we could get all the necessary papers. I wouldn't dream of jeopardizing her family's safety. She was delighted at my suggestion.

Our travel passes entailed interminable queuing at the prefecture but it was worth it. On 23 December we squeezed onto a crowded train bound for Avignon. We were met at the station by the whole family: Madame Odette, Biquet, Katia, Jean-Pierre and even Monsieur Claude, who had been invalided out of the Army. We drove to the new farm which was impressive and sat down to eat at a large table overlooking the orchard. We talked into the night, well after Katia and Jean-Pierre had been packed off to bed. Biquet was in that awkward phase of early adolescence and was quite reserved over the meal, but he finally overcame his reticence and plied us with questions about our escape. Two parts stood out for him: the hole in the wire fence behind the Casino at Vittel and our lucky find of the station hotel at Marseille, with the train inspection facing us at the end of the platform. We had to go over every inch of these stories for him.

'I think young Biquet is a little in love with you,' said Frida teasingly as we lay in bed later. 'You're the romantic prisoner of war on the run.'

'Maybe,' I replied as I rolled over to go to sleep.

I smiled to myself, remembering that during my previous time in Avignon I had always been just Patoun to Biquet, the gangly English au pair with whom he had never really got on.

The next day was Christmas Eve. We were all up early and were given tasks to do. It was obvious that months of preparation had gone into these Christmas celebrations, with carefully planned black-market dealings, cooking and storing. Friends and neighbours arrived in the early evening. About twenty of us finally sat down for the *réveillon* feast of seven courses and various wines. It was a wonderful evening, if somewhat frenetic. Between some of the courses we danced to a gramophone. Everyone was determined to enjoy themselves and to forget the anxieties and worries of the outside world. And for me there was the added joy of seeing again my French family.

'Tell us about the hole in the wire, Patoun,' said Biquet from across the table.

So Frida and I had to recount for the guests the story of our lives over the last eighteen months. As we did so I became aware for the first time that my war story, even though it was still unfinished, was already becoming a carefully edited party piece. This was a highlights-only version for people whom I hardly knew. I would probably spend the rest of my life refining it. There were hoots of laughter at our description of shuttling between brothels in Marseille, and joyful disbelief at the thought of my elegant suitcases arriving from Paris courtesy of Thomas Cook. A sombre note was struck when I described how I had watched the magnificent march of the German Army down the Champs-Elysées in June 1940.

Monsieur Claude brought out two bottles of a liqueur that he had recently started to produce from the pear trees on the farm. He sat down next to me and began to tell me of his problems. He had for sure provided lavish hospitality, yet the future was insecure for the small farmer. The supplies necessary to run a farm were restricted, many debts were unpaid and much of the farming produce went straight to Germany at rock-bottom prices. For the moment he could see no solution. As we drank more of the beautiful liqueur he became morose and cynical. I was quite relieved when the party broke up and some of us went to continue the festivities in the barn of a neighbouring farm. We danced and drank for the rest of the night.

Back in Marseille a couple of days later we found our friends were hard at work planning the New Year celebrations. For the festivities we crowded into a small cafe on the main street, the Canebière. A young Belgian artist had produced individual menus for each of us in beautiful copperplate writing. Everyone contributed to the meal, which was as sumptuous as our Christmas feast with the Manguins. It included almost unheard of luxuries such as olives, mandarins, pâté and a delicious roast rabbit as a main course. Four different wines were served. Again we danced and sang until dawn. I remember Frida and I doing a rendition of 'Roll out the Barrel' with tears in our eyes. Our friends didn't know the words but they banged their hands on the tables in accompaniment.

I think that our singing of that particular song was inspired by an amazing woman I had met soon after our arrival in Marseille. Nancy Wake (or Madame Fiocca, to use her married name) was Australian. She was a striking, fleshy woman who was only a few years older than I. She had married a wealthy Marseille steel industrialist and they had a beautiful, white flat with all mod cons on the hill overlooking the city and the harbour.

I met Nancy for the first time after being taken to her house for dinner and the two of us instantly became friends. She took us with her to the bars and cafes around the Canebière where the barmen all knew her. My favourite was a nightclub called Eden. With its soft music and plush red seating it was a haven away from war. Frida disliked it and rarely visited.

After one particularly raucous evening there, Nancy and I staggered out, linked arms and began to sing 'Rule, Britannia' in the dark streets. Frida was furious when I told her what I had done. She thought I had been foolish. But Nancy was irrepressible. On one memorable occasion, when she was incensed by some piece of war news, she stood up in the crowded little bar at the Eden, raised her glass and shouted: 'Ladies and Gentlemen, I give you the King.'

It was probably Nancy who had provided most of the luxuries for the New Year celebrations. She was incredibly generous, although her hospitality could be quite daunting if her temper was up. She would have the most spectacular rows with her husband Henri. Having grown up with the restrained tensions of silence of my own home, I found such explosions quite extraordinary. Frida and I would weather these storms by keeping our mouths shut until the pieces of broken crockery had been gathered up and the beloved dogs had come out from behind the sofa.

One day I made a jokey comment to her about the amount of food that seemed to be consumed in her house even when there were no guests around.

'You keep that trap shut, my dear,' she said. Her round jolly face suddenly looked wary.

Nancy certainly had much to hide, even from Frida and me. Late in 1940 she had met by chance a British officer on parole from the nearby Fort Saint-Jean, where he and several hundred other British servicemen had been interned by the French military authorities. Would she be able to provide hospitality to some of his friends when they visited the town? She certainly would. To Henri's initial concern, she not only fed them but used her contacts to help them escape. From there it was a logical step to be asked to set up a safe house for escaping prisoners. No wonder there was so much food at all times.

When I first met her in December 1941 she was involved in setting up resistance lines across Vichy France and helping British soldiers to escape. She was fetching, delivering, organizing, protecting and feeding British servicemen on the run. She decided that the only way to conceal these activities was to behave as normally as she could. Being Nancy, this involved going to parties, entertaining and behaving outrageously. She kept up outward appearances magnificently. At no time would anyone have suspected that there was such an enormous strain on her as we gamboled and drank in the bars. I certainly knew nothing of her clandestine activities at the time.

Inevitably the moment came (in 1943) when she too had to escape to England. After much difficulty she got to London where she was recruited by the French section of the Special Operations Executive (SOE). Parachuted back into France the following year, she operated as an agent there with her usual disregard for danger, her Maquis and Resistance exploits becoming legendary. While she was there she discovered that Henri had been arrested by the Gestapo the previous year. He had been horribly tortured, beaten until his kidneys were hanging out of his body, and finally shot. He had disclosed nothing of their activities. She was nicknamed 'The White Mouse' by the Gestapo, because of her ability to disappear when they thought they had her cornered, and was at one time their most wanted target in France. She ended the war a highly decorated hero, awarded the Croix de Guerre with Palm and Bar, the Croix de Guerre with Star, the Chevalier de Légion d'Honneur, the Médaille de la Résistance, the George Medal and the American Medal of Freedom with a Bronze Palm.

I saw her in London in 1945 on the VE Day parade, wearing a raft of medals on her chest. She was standing in a military vehicle looking out on the crowd. Suddenly she saw me, waved and shouted: 'See you tonight at Jack's! Don't I look like a Christmas tree, old girl?'

It was after the New Year celebrations that I ran into another formidable female patron, Hoytie Wiborg, who had been my saviour at the American Hospital in Paris almost two years before. As I walked slowly down to the Vieux Port one morning I heard a loud, American voice hailing me. I turned round. It was Hoytie.

'Hello, my wonderful girl. What are you doing here?'

'What are you doing here?' I demanded in return.

Hoytie was just the same: full of life, delighted to see me and to hear my story. She was very generous, treating me to a wonderful black-market meal. In the restaurant she told me for the first time all about her own extraordinary life: her wealth, her part in the artistic circles of interwar Paris and her love for other women. I never found out precisely what she was doing in Marseille. She left for Lisbon the next day.

Many years later I discovered that she had written a delightful and warm letter to my parents from Lisbon. In it she even promised that she would go the airline offices there to make reservations for our flights back to the UK. This was in an effort to expedite the granting of our Spanish and Portuguese visas. Neither of those countries, she wrote, 'want strangers admitted for an indefinite stay... owing to the food situation'. I am still grateful for her reassuring letter to my parents and for her help in Lisbon.

CHAPTER SEVENTEEN

To London

*I*t was a shock more than a joy when at last our transit visas for Spain and Portugal came through one morning in February 1942. I don't know if they were granted as a result of Hoytie's efforts but surely our French exit visas wouldn't be long in coming now? Frida and I returned from the prefecture and went to a bar, which was practically deserted at that time of day. This should have been a moment of celebration after all our months of planning, travelling and waiting but instead both of us felt curiously flat.

'Pat, I don't know what I feel about going home. I don't know if I want to. It'll be such a different world. I feel like a prisoner afraid to leave prison.'

'I agree. Remember that night in the outhouse at Vittel waiting to escape?' Frida nodded. 'Well, I had the same feeling of panic then as I have now. I don't want to leave our friends. I'll probably never see any of them again and we'll certainly never know such a strange collection of individuals.' I grimaced as I drank my coffee.

'What about Marek?' Frida looked at me with a sly grin.

I shrugged my shoulders. I couldn't even tell my closest friend how confused I was in my feelings for him. On the one hand I certainly loved him. Our few months together had been wonderful. On the other, I knew that this was the end of our relationship. I was secretly relieved that I wouldn't be the one left behind.

The last few days in Marseille were frantic as we said our goodbyes and made the final arrangements. We were going home via Spain, Portugal and Ireland. On a cold and wet Tuesday morning we gathered at the railway station. All our friends had come to see us off: amongst others I remember Marek, Nancy, Henri, Alfred, Fritz, Jean, an Iraqi doctor who had treated me for bronchitis just a week or so before, an elderly German anarchist, an Austrian Communist couple and a former deputy from the German Reichstag. They were such a disparate group, some of whom were barely on speaking terms and summed up Marseille at that time, full of tormented prejudices, lost ideals, jealousies and the desperate hope that one day they could leave. For a brief moment they were all united by the departure of the English girls.

Nancy grabbed my arm. 'Now remember, Pat, we'll have tea at Fortnum's and after that send Henri off while we do some shopping.'

Henri smiled. 'Tell them when you get back that we are waiting for them,' he said. 'And that our morale is strengthened by their pluck and daring.'

I hugged them both. Henri's parting words were very formal but so eloquent that I was to use them in a talk I gave on the Welsh border just a month later. I still have the battered carbon copy of that speech.

'Come back with the British Army!' shouted Alfred as we got on to the train with our luggage and bits and pieces. He was grinning madly and giving a punched fist salute.

Marek and I had said our farewells earlier that morning. He was standing by a station pillar watching the hugging, the kissing, the tears and the good wishes. He now approached the train, kissed me and without a word gave me a leather-bound copy of Diderot's *Jacques le fataliste et son maître*.

My thoughts were with him during the train journey. I took little interest in what was going on around me and just curled up in my corner of the carriage. Frida left me alone. As usual, she spent almost the entire journey talking to the other occupants of the train. There were a couple of French soldiers travelling to see their families. She was very buoyed up by her conversation with them. She told me later that they were fed up with the new breed of young French fascists who were taking over the armed forces.

We had a long wait at Perpignan, where we had to change trains. The proprietor of the station cafe must have overheard us speaking in English. He leant over us and spoke softly.

'There's a rumour going around that the British and American armies have landed in Brittany. Maybe the BBC news will tell us more. Wait here.'

He saw the glint of excitement in our eyes and gave us a wink. He returned to the bar and continued dealing with the few customers that were there. After a while he disappeared into the back, returning after what seemed an age. He approached our table casually to change the ashtray, whispered a dejected 'Rien' and walked away, shaking his head.

When we finally got up to leave there were only two old men sitting at the bar counter. The proprietor handed us a small bag of food.

'To England?' he said. I nodded. 'You are lucky, *Mesdemoiselles*, to go back to a country that is still fighting. *Bonne chance*.'

Just as we got to the door Frida suddenly seemed to come to a decision. 'Wait here, Pat. I need to see someone.'

With that she disappeared. She was presumably off to see a contact. I sat down again and prepared to wait. I didn't want to be involved in her politics and preferred not to know what she was doing. Eventually she returned, obviously excited but not saying anything. We boarded the train. Only after our return home did I discover that her contact had given her two cigarettes containing messages for General de Gaulle, the leader of the Free French government-in-exile in London.

As we approached the tunnel at Cerbère leading into Spain, I hung out of the window and whispered a quiet and sentimental goodbye to this much loved country where I had lived for three years. Over the border at Port Bou we found there were long customs formalities. By now I was beginning to regret my impetuous gesture of sending for my suitcases, which were heavy enough when empty, let alone when full of my things. Our bags were examined carefully. I couldn't understand much of what the officials were saying and looked curiously at their gaudy uniforms and the posters of General Franco on the walls.

For some reason they were not satisfied with us. We were taken to a cold shed and strip-searched by two fearsome women. One of the customs officers came over to the shed. He leant against the wall, languidly smoking as he watched. When the women were finally satisfied that we were not carrying any secret coded messages or military plans (or whatever it was they were looking for), they ushered us back onto the train bound for Barcelona. Just what would have happened to both of us if they had discovered the cigarette messages for the Free French in London, I don't know.

Frida was unusually silent and morose throughout the whole journey into Spain. For her this was a terrible return. She had last been here in 1937 when she had fought on the Republican side in the Spanish Civil War, driving an ambulance presented by the Scottish miners to the Frente Popular and working in a radio station. She now had to confront the new Spain of Franco. I know that she was worried in case the authorities somehow checked up on her past activities. She might be detained here indefinitely as an undesirable.

I had not been to Spain before and did not know what to expect but I was still shocked at what I found as we came into Barcelona. The city was in ruins, with bombed buildings everywhere. As soon as we got off the train we were accosted by ragged, hungry people with fear in their eyes as they quietly begged for money.

Mr Randall had told us in Marseille to make our way immediately to the British Consulate. He had assured us that they would arrange everything for our return to England. It was on our arrival at the Consulate, however, that the trouble started. Admittedly, we didn't quite have the look of guests at a garden party. I, in particular, must have been a real sight: dressed in a headscarf and shabby clothes, I was struggling with my two large suitcases and matching hatbox. But we certainly did not expect to be blocked by the porter at the entrance and ushered brusquely like tradesmen around to the side, despite a large notice quite visible behind him directing people through the hall to the British Repatriation Office.

After a short wait we were shown into a small office and met by a pompous consular official who neither smiled at nor greeted us. Dressed in a gentlemanly pin-stripe suit, he listened to our story in undisguised distaste and examined our passports carefully. He was out of the room for quite a while, presumably conferring with a colleague, and he returned with an official-looking form and a wad of pesetas.

'Well, young ladies, I have the names of a couple of good hotels here. You shouldn't have a problem in getting a room for the night.' He wrote the details of two hotels on a scrap of paper and handed it to us.

'We'd like to get you to Madrid as soon as possible,' he continued, without looking up. 'On tomorrow night's train, preferably. You're both bona fide British citizens, so our people there can arrange your onward travel to England. Now, if you would just sign here to say that you have received money from us.'

We signed his form without bothering to read it. He ushered us to the door as if hurrying to be rid of us.

'The sleeper to Madrid has very good first-class couchettes, I think you'll find. Oh, as for refunding the money, that will be arranged by HMG as soon as you reach London. Goodbye.'

Perhaps these parting remarks about London were his supercilious way of comforting us. If this was their intention, then they had the opposite effect upon Frida. I could see her trembling with anger, her pent-up distress at being back in Spain barely under the surface. She turned to the official with an icy stare.

'We've managed to get this far travelling third class. That's how we mean to continue. Goodbye.'

We both burst out laughing when we got outside. At the station we found that we would, in fact, have to wait a couple of days before we could get tickets for the Madrid train. Ignoring the recommendations of the dreadful official, we booked in at the Hotel Internacional, an old and noisy place in the middle of the city.

We deposited our luggage there and went out to see Barcelona. La Rambla, the wide street running down the centre to the port, was crowded and colourful, with the first spring flowers on sale. The shops were full of food. If a visitor could ignore the bomb damage that was all around, they might easily think that life here was not nearly as depressing as in France. We soon realized, however, that the prices were exorbitant. It was difficult to imagine how the ordinary citizen could afford to buy anything.

We had a meal in a large restaurant down by the port. It was delicious and cost the earth. Still, we were saving money by staying in a cheap hotel and not travelling first class. But by the end of the meal we were both uncomfortable and wanted to leave: people were constantly coming to the window of the restaurant and simply staring at what we were eating.

We had to wait around in the city for two days. We were both quite subdued in our moods. I think that Frida was finding it very disturbing being back in Spain. While for my part, I simply wanted to be on the move again homewards. We stayed quietly at the hotel for most of the time, sitting on our beds reading. On the second day we made an excursion to a park on a hill from where you could look down on the whole city.

That night we had a long and very uncomfortable journey to Madrid. Our reception on arrival at the British Embassy the following morning was as frosty as the one in Barcelona. Again the porter looked somewhat aghast at our bedraggled clothes and luggage as we tried to enter the main door. He seemed reluctant to allow us inside the building at all.

At least this time, however, the official dealing with us was friendlier than the pompous ass in Barcelona. She was a young woman who could not have been much older than I. We were again given a daily allowance by the embassy on the promise that we would repay every penny on our return to England. They arranged for us to stay at a rather fine place called the Hotel Mora. We decided not to raise any objections to their choice.

I hoped against hope that we could leave this sad country as quickly as possible. We knew from the embassy that we would have to wait a few days before we could get a train to Portugal. But how many? Train tickets were precious because of the shortage of coal and the damage to rolling stock as a result of the Civil War.

One important thing that the British officials here and in Barcelona failed to do was to inform their superiors in London that we had arrived in Spain. We didn't know this at the time. The result of this failure in communication had alarming results for our parents. During our stay in Marseille we had tried to stagger our weekly letters or telegrams home so that one set of parents would receive news every few days. They were regularly on the telephone to one another to swap the latest details. All communications from us ceased in late February, of course, when we left Marseille.

Our parents were desperately worried at the sudden silence on our part. We had told them that we were leaving to go home via Spain but for an anxious couple of weeks they had no idea if we were safe. Nobody in Whitehall seemed to know where we were. Many years later I found my father's frantic letters from this time to every official contact he could think of, trying to find out what had happened.

Our brief stay in Madrid was as sad as I had feared that morning when we arrived. We spent one day squashed in a crowded train going to Toledo. It was an extraordinary contrast to step out of the poverty all around us and see the sheer beauty of the cathedral with its wonderful El Grecos and fabulous treasures. The sacristan who showed us round explained how careful everyone had been during the fighting not to damage the treasures which had been buried underground in safe hiding places. He was a small, unhappy man who kept shaking our hands and bemoaning the state of Spain.

'There is so much misery, so much cruelty, so much intrigue. Even here in Toledo there are spies and people denouncing one another. *Una tragedia, señoritas.*' We could only agree, especially when we saw the ruins of the Alcázar. This had once been the finest Moorish building in Spain and was now rubble.

To our great relief the train tickets for Lisbon came through the next day. We chose to go third class and pocketed for other purposes the first-class train money again supplied by HMG, reasoning that we were borrowing the money and could therefore do whatever we wanted with it. We made our journey to the border jammed tight on wooden slat seats. The windows were firmly shut against the cold evening air. There was an overpowering smell of garlic and rancid oil building up in this unventilated atmosphere.

'Frida, for once no more tragic war stories on this journey, if you don't mind.'

She nodded vaguely in agreement. We had made our introductions to our fellow passengers and were by now all sharing food and drink. But I could see that Frida was itching to get away and talk to other passengers about the Civil War, bringing the harrowing stories back to me.

'Why don't we have some music,' I quickly suggested, trying to forestall her.

She agreed and we asked our companions to sing some songs. They did this with great gusto and much handclapping and finger-clicking for the flamenco tunes. A rather wizened old man in the corner seemed to have an inexhaustible supply of cold red wine for the compartment. It was all rather jolly. At last the large woman sitting opposite (who didn't seem to have a tooth in her head) beckoned to me to sing: 'Canción inglesa, canción inglesa.'

I tried to think of something suitable and gave a rather feeble rendition of 'Early One Morning'. Frida followed with 'Drink To Me Only'. While we were both good violinists we had rather weak voices. Our efforts were met with polite and muted applause. We seemed to have succeeded in deflating the febrile atmosphere of the carriage in about five minutes flat.

'A sea shanty,' I whispered to Frida. 'That'll restore English prestige!' I was right. We started with 'What Shall We Do With The Drunken Sailor?' and carried on with 'Blow the Man Down'. I was by now inspired and launched into 'Spanish Ladies'. Soon even the old man with the wine was humming away with us.

At the border we said our goodbyes. We were pleased that after the sadness of our journey through Spain we were leaving that country laughing and singing with our Spanish fellow travellers. We then had more lengthy immigration and customs formalities to face, including another strip-search, but at last we boarded a train bound for Lisbon. We journeyed through a land that seemed to have stopped in time. Peasants in colourful clothes went barefoot in the fields. Muleteers ambled along wearing capes of a deep blue. The villages were bright, clean and toy-like in the sunshine.

Once in Lisbon we again went to the British Consulate with its ubiquitous British Repatriation Office. A nervous man attended to us. He had a sheaf of official papers in front of him.

'We've been expecting you. And in fact, Miss Say, your father has already arranged payment for your air fares to the United Kingdom.'

'That's wonderful,' I said with a broad smile. 'When do we go?'

He shook his head. 'I'm afraid that payment doesn't guarantee you a definite seat.'

'But you'll surely be able to get us on a plane soon?'

'Hopefully,' he said, looking rather uncomfortable. 'Now, I'll advance you some money. And we have arranged for you to stay at this hotel.' He handed me a small card with the name 'Nova Pensão Camoes' printed on it.

I was rather taken aback by the whole interview. I had half-guessed that my father had been beavering away on my behalf, probably since war had been declared over two years before. I recalled that he had contacted the British Consul in Marseille back in 1940 just before the Germans had overrun France, in an effort to get me out of the country. But I had hardly expected to arrive in Lisbon to find the last leg of our journey already sewn up by him courtesy of BOAC!

It was not until after his death in 1958, when we were sorting out his papers, that I realized the full extent of my father's efforts on our behalf in those months. He was to tell me very little about his activities after my return to London. That was his way. Among his papers I came across a large buff envelope marked 'Pat's Journey'. It was full of carbon copies of letters sent to a whole range of organizations – the Red Cross, various US and British government ministries, banks and airlines. From his desk at the Admiralty he had excelled himself in writing to everyone with the tiniest bit of influence asking them to do what they could for me. I discovered that not only had he paid over £72 for our airfares from Lisbon (nearly £3,000 in today's money), but he had also persuaded the Air Ministry in London to give us some form of priority for our air passages back to the United Kingdom. He and Frida's father had both given written assurances that we were anxious to get back to Britain in order to join up.

He had stoical perseverance on my behalf. One letter to a colleague at the Admiralty told of his delight that:

... you have been able to obtain some firm news of your boy ... [that] ... means so much to worried wives and mothers in these distressful days. Unfortunately we still have no news of our two girls waiting at Marseilles for repatriation.

Just a few days later, with the information that we were on our way home, another Admiralty colleague wrote: 'What grand news and may I soon catch up and find myself able to tell you equally good tidings of my stepson.' There was an element of gentle one-upmanship in all this correspondence which made me laugh and cry as I read it that evening at my parents' home.

Not long after the discovery of all my father's patient work I spoke to Shula about her father's activities during her imprisonment. She told me that after her arrest in Paris as a British national, he had gone every day to their local police station to ask for news of his daughter. He had subsequently disappeared to his death in a concentration camp. Both our fathers had cared deeply in their own ways and in their own vastly different circumstances.

Frida and I had five days in Lisbon and we were able to unwind a little. It was early March and already quite warm. As in Madrid, the shops were full of expensive food and goods which ordinary people couldn't begin to afford. But apart from that, the contrast with this city was startling: quite simply, there was none of the detritus of war. Even under their dictatorial regime, the people here seemed to be more relaxed than anywhere else we had been.

We were busy for all five nights. On the Sunday evening we were invited to a dance given by a Galician Club where the members came from the north of Spain. Frida was particularly interested to hear the songs and see the dances of this little-known part of the country. She was doomed to disappointment: the young people, all dressed in their best Europeanized clothes, were only interested in jazz and swing.

The other nights we were wined and dined extravagantly by consular officials. For the first time, language was a barrier for us, although Frida seemed to manage by gabbling 'Spanish like a Cockney with a cold,' as she put it.

It was all very pleasant but I began to wonder if this slightly unreal socializing might not begin to wear a bit thin if we had to wait as long for an aeroplane seat as we had done in Marseille for permission to continue our journey. I sent a card to Marek, and Frida and I posted the numerous letters that our friends in Marseille had given us. We also made fruitless enquiries on their behalf at the various relief organizations.

Up to now my thoughts had been dominated by the desire to get home. I had thought little about actually living again in wartime England. Walking down from the hotel one day I noticed an office marked Distressed British Subjects' Charity Shop. Half an hour later I came out loaded down with shoes, pyjamas, coats, silk nighties, jumpers and trousers. I had spent just about every penny saved from our third-class travel on luxuries for friends, family and me. Later that day I even bought a pineapple! I was determined to show my father, in particular, that I hadn't made a mess of things by staying in France after war was declared.

As it turned out, there was no need to worry about being stuck in Lisbon. At midnight on 9 March we made our way to the airport at Cintra. I thankfully shed my mounds of luggage at the check-in. We walked out in the darkness to the runway, guided by torchlight. As we approached the steps of the camouflaged and blacked-out aeroplane Frida pointed at the next berth. It was a Lufthansa. I could make out some German words being shouted.

This was my first flight and I found the whole experience marvellously glamorous. We tried to find a chink at the windows so that we could see the last of the Lisbon lights before total darkness engulfed us but the blackout precautions were too good. Despite the noise from the engines, I slept soundly for a few hours. It was in a very misty dawn that we finally stepped off the plane and quickly piled into a coach to drive for some time before disembarking at a large and rather ramshackle hotel in a remote Irish village.

We were treated to a wonderful breakfast: eggs, bacon, sausages, warm brown soda bread and my first taste of black pudding. I was flabbergasted by the food available, although this was perhaps understandable in a neutral country. I wondered idly how long it would be before I saw, let alone ate, some of these things again.

Frida and I wandered around after breakfast. We were in Adare, a charming model village set in rich agricultural land quite near to Limerick. Leaving Frida, I made straight for the few clothes shops. Their windows were full of good material, including tweeds and woollens. Unlike Madrid and Lisbon, the prices were affordable and all without the dreaded clothing coupons I had heard so much about in letters from my mother. At John Smith's little drapery store I bought socks, stockings, a jumper, knitting wool (twenty-eight balls), tweed and even darning wool! The receipt read: £3. 13s. 4d.

Frida and I were half-expecting to be looked on by the local populace with suspicion or even hostility. After all, we were a strange group of English people and Ireland was not on our side in this conflict. Indeed, it had been at war with us just twenty years before. I remembered how the people of Besançon had been told we were spies; and again in Vittel the word had gone round that we were German women staying at the spa for convalescence.

We encountered, in fact, a gentle warmth from the people of the village. I had a long conversation with the owner of a bar-cum-shop who was delighted to discover that my parents' house (that I was now returning to) was just a mile away from where his brother lived in Cricklewood, North London. I had my first taste of Guinness there and he would not let me pay for it.

There must have been about thirty of us encamped at the hotel. We were a mixed bag but we were used to that by now: embassy and consular staff on leave, naval officers from Gibraltar and three distinctly rich ladies in furs whom I never managed to engage in conversation. Indeed, once they ascertained I couldn't make up a fourth at bridge they barely looked at me. One of the officers had been at Cambridge with my brother. We talked at length after dinner but it was rather hard going. The only topics he was interested in were his undergraduate days and the ballerina Margot Fonteyn.

We were taken by launch to a seaplane bobbing about in the water. It was the first and last time that I ever flew in this exciting form of transport. Take-off and descent were like some great bird whooshing through the water with its wings spread. At last, after so many months of travel, we arrived back in England. We landed at Poole Harbour, where Frida and I faced intense questioning and form-filling. We were considered with some suspicion until the authorities had satisfied themselves that our stories were indeed true. In my particular case, they kept on coming back to the fact that I had gone up to Paris just as the Germans were about to arrive. Why?

We were interrogated separately for over six hours. In a cold, drab, darkened room I faced a young captain in the Intelligence Corps who questioned me in the tone of voice which implied 'You won't be able to answer that one!' I was given cups of tepid tea and invited to tell the truth, the whole truth and nothing but the truth. The only thing missing was the Bible. After an exhausting session (I remember his ashtray full of cigarette butts) he suddenly seemed to make a decision about me.

'Well,' he said as he put his papers together. 'That all appears to be correct and above board. I suppose you know that you will have to refund the money advanced to you. And, of course, you'll be getting your call-up papers at once.'

Finally, Frida and I were put on a train for Waterloo. We arrived to find a huge group of family, friends and the press all waiting for us. To our delight, we made the front page of the London *Evening Standard* that night with a large picture of us smiling. We were good propaganda value. As the reporter wrote, we stepped off the train as if we were 'just back from a Continental holiday . . . with big suitcases and string bags filled with pineapples and other good things from Lisbon.'

It was 14 March 1942. Precisely one year, nine months and three days since I had left Avignon to go home.

Epilogue

Frida and I had a hectic time during the first weeks following our arrival. I wrote this in a letter to Marek just four weeks after my return:

> Since we arrived back at the station we haven't had a moment's rest. Reporters, articles in several newspapers, photographs – the whole caboodle. We've given a number of talks on radio and addressed meetings.

Curiously the British authorities left us totally alone and I was never fully debriefed in London. My long interrogation on arrival at Poole had been merely to satisfy them that I was a bona fide British escapee. Nobody in authority in London, however, seemed to have the slightest interest in the fact that I had recent and intimate knowledge of both Vichy and Occupied France.

Once the initial flurry of excitement had subsided I had what must have been a delayed reaction to my experiences. I started to become emotionally very volatile: from giddy excitement to deep depression almost overnight. I was constantly tired. Many weekends were spent almost entirely in bed. In those days there was no counselling or therapy to help me to cope with any after-effects of my ordeal. I was left to get on with life.

What was I going to do with myself now that I was back in England? I didn't really know. I expected to get my call-up papers anytime in those first few weeks. One thing was certain: I flatly refused to go into military uniform and live behind the barbed wires of a camp again, even if this time I would be allowed to walk through its gates as and when I wanted. My father, perhaps sensing my distress, arranged for me to go for an office job at the Admiralty, but I left the building without a word just before I was called in for interview. He never mentioned the incident afterwards.

In the early summer of 1942 I heard on the grapevine that there was an outfit in central London called the Special Operations Executive or SOE, which was involved in clandestine operations in Occupied Europe. I wrote to them and outlined my background. Within a few days I received a reply from the head of their French section, a Colonel Maurice Buckmaster, inviting me to present myself for interview at their offices in Baker Street.

Just as I had been clear that I didn't want to go into the armed forces, I was equally certain that I didn't want to become an agent. I made this point forcefully at the interview. I was all too willing to help in the struggle against Germany, so long as this did not involve my returning to France. Understandably, I was viewed by SOE as prime agent material, given my knowledge of the country and its language. But I had no intention of going back there. I had lived in a France controlled by the Germans for nearly two years – from their triumphal victory in June 1940 until my departure in February 1942. I had been incarcerated and had escaped. That was enough for me. I wanted an office job.

I worked at SOE for the rest of the war. Technically I was a secretary but in reality I was a general dogsbody in the French section. I sometimes took agents to restaurants in the tense days before their departure for France, spent many an hour stamping on new French currency to make it appear old and even did some pretty disastrous coding work.

I returned to Spain in 1943, where I worked for a year attached to the SOE team at the British Embassy in Madrid. A lot of our time was spent dealing with British service personnel who had escaped from France into neutral Spain. We effectively 'bought' agents from the Spanish officials who were holding them. I remember getting particularly annoyed with two agents in San Sebastian in the north of Spain. They had been too unfit to cross the Pyrenees and had thereby endangered their helpers. But they were oblivious of this fact and spent the entire car journey to Madrid complaining about everyone and everything.

To my secret delight, my work took me several times to the British Consulate in Barcelona. Before my first visit I spent ages dressing myself as smartly as I could. I entered through the front door very slowly and deliberately. I was determined to savour the very real and satisfying thrill of walking past the condescending official who had so smoothly directed Frida and myself in our tattered clothes to the side entrance the year before.

After a year of hard work and strenuous social life I left Spain to go back to London. It wasn't the most glorious of exits. I had fallen in love with a Spaniard called Ricardo. During the week he was the head porter at the hotel where I had first stayed and on Sundays he was a moderately successful bullfighter. My superiors at the embassy considered that this was not appropriate behaviour for a British diplomatic official. I was returned to England to work again at SOE's Baker Street offices for the last few months of its existence, with the legendary Vera Atkins as my boss.

At least the British Government paid for my ignominious return from Spain. It had to: I was a British diplomat. But the government was still chasing me for money I owed from my repatriation. This battle over my debt was to drag on until 1947.

It had taken me about four months to get from Marseille to England during the winter of 1941–42. During that time I had been advanced money (in order to live) by the US Consul in Marseille and British consular officials in Barcelona, Madrid and Lisbon. My father had paid both mine and Frida's air fares of £36.0s.6d. each from Lisbon to Poole.

The Foreign Office presented me with its final assessment of my debt about a year after my return. They calculated that I owed them precisely £64.1s.9d. (or over £2,500 in today's money.) Of this, £39 corresponded to my time in Marseille; presumably the Americans had asked for their money back too.

I failed to see why I should have to pay HMG anything. After all, whose fault was it that I had ended up in Paris just a couple of days before the Germans arrived in June 1940? I pointed out to the Foreign Office that I had been badly advised at the time by the British Consulate in Marseille. They had urged me to go northwards and slip through to St-Malo. I wrote: 'It cannot be denied that had the British Consul advised me to remain in Marseille, I would most certainly have been able to leave the city.'

The Foreign Office would have none of this. The question of repayment, they replied, could only be waived on the grounds of destitution. What were my financial circumstances and what could I afford to pay by monthly instalments?

I ignored a number of letters on this score. In September 1943, much to my indignation, I was warned that they would take legal action. We eventually reached a settlement. I was to make an immediate payment of £6, followed by contributions of £1 per month, starting in October. This I duly did and thereafter I received a little letter every month from the Under-Secretary of State for Foreign Affairs, who presented his compliments and acknowledged my cheque for £1.

I was still bitterly resentful that I had to pay the full cost of my escape and that no recognition had been given of what I had done or had been through. I was by now working as a secretary to Tom Driberg, the Labour MP. In that capacity I had come into contact on several occasions with a very helpful official at the Foreign Office – a Mr Guy Burgess. I wrote to him, requesting that the remaining debt be written off. I couldn't help adding the gratuitously insulting comment that had I escaped as a member of the armed forces and not as a private citizen I would probably have been presented with an MBE and not a bill!

A few days later I received a reply from Mr Burgess. He had made enquiries, he wrote, and had found that I had made a good effort at

(X13397/313/501)

FOREIGN OFFICE,
8, Carlton House Terrace,
S.W. 1.

17th December, 1947.

Dear Miss Say,

Thank you for your letter of the 27th November, about your repatriation in 1942.

I have made enquiries and find that the balance still due by you is £18. 5. 7. Since you have made such a good effort at repayment by regular instalments and now find it difficult to pay more it is agreed that the claim for the balance will be waived.

Yours sincerely,

G. Burgess.

(G. Burgess)

Miss R. Say,
Private Secretary to
Mr. T. Driberg, M.P.
House of Commons.

repayment. As I was now in financial difficulties, the Foreign Office would be prepared to waive the balance of £18.5s.7d.

A few years later, when Guy Burgess was exposed as a Soviet spy and defected to the Soviet Union, I briefly thought about selling his autographed letter but decided against it. After all, I had at least managed to get him to cough up the princely sum of £18.5s.7d!

Rosie's Journey

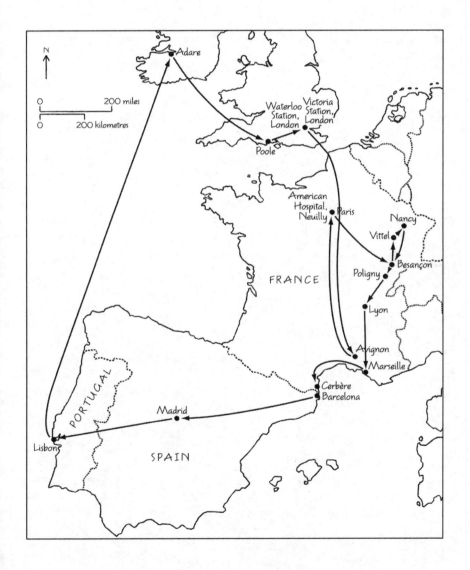

What Happened Next

*F*rida worked in London during the war for General de Gaulle's Free French organization. She later married a microbiologist and had four children. She remained a committed Communist all her life, wrote a number of books on music and the French Resistance and was a life-long member of CND. She died in 1996.

Shula remained at the Vittel camp until its liberation. She married a fellow artist and had two children. They moved to Brittany where she still lives and paints.

Père Manguin, the head of the Manguin family, died in 1949. His daughter, Lucile, became a very celebrated couturier in Paris after the war. Biquet, the boy I used to take to school on my oversize bicycle, owns a guesthouse in Avignon.

Madame Izard was soon reunited with her husband, Georges. He joined the Resistance and had a brilliant postwar career as a barrister. I kept in contact with her for many years after the war and we became good friends, with the younger members of our family doing language-exchange visits. Christophe, who as a small child would accompany me on my daily visits to the *Kommandantur* in Paris, later became a celebrated television producer.

Marek got away from Marseille in April 1942. He sent me a telegram from America of just one word: 'Safe.' He enlisted in the US

Army the following year. The last time I heard from him was a letter in late 1943 from 'somewhere in England'.

Hoytie Wiborg arrived safely in America not long after I got back to England. I received a kind letter from her in May of that year; the headed notepaper was (appropriately) from one of the Vanderbilt mansions on Fifth Avenue, New York. I never heard from her again. She died in 1964.

Nancy Wake went back to Australia after the war. On the death of her second husband, she settled in the Stafford Hotel in London, selling her collection of medals to finance her stay. For the past few years she has been at a home for ex-service people in Richmond, West London, financially supported (according to press reports) by Prince Charles.

Sofka Skipworth was released from the camp at Vittel in 1944. She returned to work for Laurence Olivier after the war. She remained a committed Communist, retiring to Bodmin Moor in Cornwall. I would see her from time to time when I visited my sister, Joan, who lived near by. Her life story, *Sofka: The Autobiography of a Princess*, was published in 1968 by Hart-Davis.

Mr Sutton sent me a charming letter in August 1945. He was by now at the British Consulate General in Strasbourg. He wrote: 'As you may observe . . . I survived.'

The Caserne Vauban at Besançon continued as a military camp until just a few years ago. It now belongs to the municipality of Besançon, which plans to redevelop the seven-acre site as a housing complex. It is in a derelict condition and seems to be a favoured place for local youths to hold (unauthorized) parties.

The Vittel camp was used in the latter stages of the war to house Jewish prisoners en route to almost certain death in concentration camps in Germany and Poland. It was liberated by the Allies in September 1944. The Grand Hotel is now part of the Club Med organization.

After leaving SOE, Rosie worked first for the Labour MP Tom Driberg and then for the editor of the *New Statesman*, Kingsley Martin. She later became a professional journalist and was for many years a theatre critic at *The Sunday Telegraph* and the *Financial Times*. She was married twice: first to the political journalist Ian Mackay, who died in 1952, and then to the newspaper and BBC journalist Julian Holland, by whom she had two children. She stayed a North London girl all her life and, after her divorce from Julian, lived in Primrose Hill until her death in1996.

Picture Acknowledgements

Thanks to David Woodroffe
for the wonderful illustrations on pages 61, 176 and 245.

Thanks to Jimmy Knight for permission to use the evocative sketches
by his mother Frida on pages 112, 117, 122, 123, 127 and 128.

Thanks also to the following agencies who supplied images
for the plate section.

Page 6: (top) Guerre 1939–1945. Besançon.
Camp d'internés civils. Vue des immeubles.
© Photothèque CICR (DR) (Image reference: V-P-HIST-E-00793)

Page 7: (bottom) Mémorial de la Shoah/CDJC

Page 8: (top) Mémorial de la Shoah/CDJC

INDEX

Index Note: Rosemary Say is abbreviated to RS in parts of the index. Where the full names of people have not been included in the book an identifying note in parenthesis has been added to their entry.

WAR ORGANISATION
OF THE
BRITISH RED CROSS SOCIETY and ORDER OF ST. JOHN OF JERUSALEM

FOREIGN RELATIONS DEPARTMENT

Director :
THE RT. HON. THE EARL OF CLARENDON. K.G.. G.C.M.G.. G.C.V.O.

Assistant Deputy Directors :
LADY ENID BROWNE
MISS MARY CAMPION, O.B.E.
MISS HELEN McSWINEY

Deputy Director :
MISS S. J. WARNER, O.B.E.

TELEPHONE NO.:
ABBEY 2511/5

PLEASE QUOTE REF.

ESB/JM B/B

WARWICK HOUSE,
ST. JAMES'S, LONDON. S.W.1

17th December, 1940.

Richard Say, Esq.,
42, Pattison Road,
Hampstead, N.W.2.

Dear Mr. Say,

re: Miss Rosemary Say

In reply to your letter of the 12th
we have written to the International Red C
mittee in Geneva asking them to try and fin
whether your daughter has been receiving as
for the past five months from the American C
in Paris who, as you know, has had instructio
give the necessary financial aid to British s
requiring it. We feel quite sure t
daughter has registered
she will b

Notes for persons wishing to commun
friends in Enemy Countries, or Territory in the
occupation of the Enemy.

Authority has been given to permit communication with persons
in enemy territories, subject to the following conditions.

The territories included in these arrangements are: Belgium, Czechoslovakia, Danzig, Denmark, France (German-occupied), Germany, Holland,
Italy and Italian Possessions, Luxembourg, Norway, Poland (German-occupied)
and the Channel Islands.

1. Communications must be brief. Erasures are not permitted.
2. Letters must omit the sender's address. They may be in English or in the
of the country for which they are intended (except Czech), and
tain nothing but matters of personal interest.
eference may be made to any town, village, locality or journey in
itain, to any phase of the war, or to Thos. Cook & Son, Ltd., or
heir offices. No enclosure of the following nature is permitted:
matter, map, plan, sketch, drawing, print, photograph, or other
representation, or postage or revenue stamp.
ness letters and letters containing directions about property or
atters must not be sent to Thos. Cook & Son, Ltd., but should be
d by the sender to the Trading with the Enemy Branch of the
and Board of Trade, Imperial House, Kingsway, London, W.C.
ter must be placed in an open unstamped envelope fully inscribed
addressee, who should be asked to address any reply to your full
are of Post Box 506, LISBON (Lissabon in the case of letters from
y or German-occupied territory), Portugal.
en envelope containing the letter should be placed in an outer
envelope and sent to Thos. Cook & Son, Ltd., Berkeley Street,
ly, London, W.1., together with a memorandum, plainly written,
ing in block characters the name and full address of the sender,
open addressed envelope for the forwarding of a reply, should one
ived from the correspondent.
mmunication to Thos. Cook & Son, Ltd., must enclose Postal Order
2s. (stamps or International Coupons cannot be accepted), which
l cover the postage of one envelope containing one communication
neutral country, and from the neutral country to the addressee,
a reply (if any) from the neutral country to Messrs. Cook's Head
London, and from that office to the intended recipient. The fee
postage of the reply from enemy territory to

Miss Freda Stewart (left),
with her companion, Miss
Rosemary Say.

E · H · GOMBRICH

THE STORY
OF ART

PHAIDON

VELAZQUEZ: *Las Meninas*. Painted in 1656. Madrid, Prado

The scene is the Court Painter's studio, where Velazquez is engaged on a portrait of the King and Queen. We must imagine the royal pair outside the picture where we are, and seeing what we see: their own reflection in the distant mirror, the painter at work and the welcome visit of their little daughter, the Infanta Margarita, who has been brought to the studio with her Maids of Honour, (*Meninas*), her tutors and her dwarfs, to pay her respects and relieve the boredom of the sitting.